AMERICA'S MANIFEST DESTINY

AMERICA'S MANIFEST DESTINY

AN ANCIENT INSCRIPTION REVEALS A CLARION CALL TO ACTION

Robert E. Mawire

Leavitt Peak Press

ISBN: 978-1-967361-29-8 (sc)
ISBN: 978-1-967361-30-4 (e)

Rev. date: 04/15/2025

DEDICATION

To the Holy One of Israel who set America apart as a beacon of light to the nations.

CONTENTS

ACKNOWLEDGMENTS

I am deeply indebted to the countless faceless, nameless, ordinary people who impacted me by the preeminence of their qualitative change in the last two decades.

It was obvious that this present epoch is one of critical moments as evidenced by the existential struggle of the poor, the hedonistric values of the super-rich, the apostatized church, corporate corruption, the nightmarish living in the American ghetto and the post 9/11 global war on terror.

This book constitutes collective insights, influence, impressions and in-depth analyses of the present cultural cold war and the sounds and echoes of the collision of cultures and the distant war in the Middle East.

I could not help but question the causes and effects of these convulsions. I looked to ordinary people and history for answers to our national dilemma as history often repeats itself. As I listened to everyday folks, I found that common sense still exists among common people. The common answer they gave me was that the present convulsions are the combustion of our pride and the eddies of the backwash of spiritual apostasy and the denial of America's Manifest Destiny. I want to express my greater gratitude to these silent voices of the masses, who still believe America is one nation under God.

I am thankful for the courageous cadre of "all American" writers who resisted the secular revision of America's providential history, at the risk of losing their reputation and jobs, to deliver the truth to future generations.

I especially appreciate the Americans brave men and women who laid the ultimate sacrifice for everything that is beautiful about America, the liberation of Europe from Nazism and global communism and for the liberation and democratization of many oppressed third-world countries worldwide.

From the beginning of the research and the writing of this book, I realized that this writing could be the most controversial and contradictive to the historical myth about the New World as well as an explosive challenge to the politically correct doctrine of pluralism which is a distinct peculiarity of our present day culture.

I am grateful for my sons Jonathan, Caleb and Stephen, for their inspiration and invaluable contribution to this work. I engaged my brilliant and street-smart boys in heated lively debates and analyses of the complex questions facing our nation I benefited a lot from their quantitative youthful perception and insights that inherently reflected the ethos and attributes of their generation.

I owe so much to the cumulative contribution of the WRNO Worldwide short wave radio family's dedication and commitment to the urgent task of taking the good news to the whole world to fulfill America's Manifest Destiny. They are a microcosm of everything that is beautiful about America. The America of Divine Manifest destiny is a chosen people, set apart to show forth His glory; a city built upon a hill. The America of the Founding Fathers is an America worth fighting for.

Most of all I am indebted to my wife Janet, as we collaborated together to bring this book into being. It never ceases to amaze me how she weaves a seamless day, multitasking effectively, efficiently, lovingly and unselfishly in spite of her many demands as a mother and a professional woman. She retyped and reshaped the manuscripts countless times, cheerfully and prayerfully.

Above all, I would like to acknowledge the grace of God and His inspiration, without which I could have never been able to write this book.

Finally, my prayers are that the readers of this book will sense the impending danger that is confronting our nation and act before it is too late. It is time to heed an ancient wise saying, "It is better to light a candle than to curse the darkness." Brighten the corner where you are.

Robert Mawire

Chapter One

PROVIDENCE

The question is, "who made America great?" The preeminence of America is not coincidental. She did not rise to sole superpower by her own bootstraps and self-reliance, but by divine providence. God opened for her the avalanches of abundance, impregnated her with vision and lavished her with unlimited blessings. She enjoys the highest quality of life over this side of eternity.

God raised America for a definitive and specific purpose: to be a lighthouse in a dark world. This much is certain, America has no future apart from her God-given destiny. If America is to survive, she must reject the revisionists who deny America's providential history.

Most of the rejectionists are evolutionists who deny that God created the heavens and the earth. They embrace an unproven and unsubstantiated evolutionary theory that dilutes man's dignity. Human origin is the crux of the matter; if there is no God then nothing matters. America is self-made. We have to defeat this despicable plot to deny America's Manifest Destiny, which is being cunningly crafted by a diabolical cabal that rejects God.

The overriding and overwhelming fact is that God created man in His own image. He is the absolute controller of the affairs of man. He is the Lord of history. This is a fact so obvious and so universal that only a "fool can say there is no God." History bears irrefutable evidence, throughout the last 6000 years of written human history, that God raises empires and casts them down when they become rebellious.

> *"He changes times and seasons; he deposes kings and rises up others. He gives wisdom to the wise and knowledge to the discerning." Daniel 2:21*

God established the age of America in the Jubilee year 1776. Her greatness is providential. America is more than its institutions, but its faith. The union was born out of the great reawakening that united the people and homogenized them into one people—one nation under God—with one faith in the Lord Jesus from coast to coast. It is our shared Judeo-Christian values that unite us. The Protestant work ethic embedded in the American culture precipitated amazing inventions and innovations. America is the cauldron of change.

The idea that "all men are created equal" is an American idea rooted in the Holy Scriptures. It is dominantly in America that the autonomous individual is celebrated. We have a Biblical understanding that, though we are created equal, we are also created unique. America values unity with diversity. This is a divine idea since it is God's prerogative to protect diversity and individuality. Christianity shaped the framework of the American idealism of capitalism with compassion and freedom. This is a biblical blueprint for national success. Most of the rest of the world is caught up in a struggle between the individual and the collective group thinking. People who deviate from the norm and think outside of the box, in many countries, are killed.

The founding fathers envisioned a land separated unto God where the individual is free to choose a path towards fulfilling his personal American dream of life, liberty and pursuit of happiness without government interference.

There is no doubt that America, as a result of this freedom, is a global economic epicenter of consumerism with the highest standard of living. The American people feel blessed with abundance by God.

There exists amazing, indisputable and solid evidence that there is a startling, direct correlation between American spirituality and its national prosperity. Ancient Israel is America's blueprint. The incisive parallelism between Israel and America which we are going to explore is in the pages of this book is amazing.

It goes without saying that, when Israel turned her back on God, she was destroyed and scattered among the nations for 2000 years. This weighs heavily on my mind; America is not exempt from the judgment of God. America reached the pinnacle of power by the grace of God, but she is falling from grace.

The collapse of America, from a position of divine favor as a sole superpower, will have an enormous impact on every nation on earth. When America goes, so goes the whole world.

America is turning her back on God. She is going the way of the bygone empires that forgot God.

> *"The wicked shall be turned into hell, and all the nations that forget God." Psalm 9:17*

She is living on borrowed time. The forces of darkness are working to remove God's favor and protection from her and to reduce this great nation into a struggling nothing. The shift of power has already be- gun as countries like China and Russia are rising to replace America. They are already pushing her to the sidelines as they see America retreating from being a world leader. She is sliding into obscurity; her influence is waning and nearing oblivion.

In the past 240 years, America served as a defender of the oppressed and protector of human rights worldwide with no strings attached. She is the hope of the faceless, nameless masses in distant lands, look- ing for a big brother.

The power shift in the global village is not coincidental—it is planned. So is the demise of the American dollar as a global reserve currency. There is a carefully planned agenda to dismantle individualism, capitalism and biblical Christianity. One-world totalitarianism is emerging to replace democracy, free-enterprise capitalism with one world economy, cash with cashless society, nation states with one world government and Christianity with one world religion.

It is crucial to recognize that, if America is cast down, when the smoke clears, we will be shocked by the perils of the collapse of America as a sole superpower. The whole world will be enslaved and oppressed with no one to turn to for help.

There exists today a mystical, sensual, seductive and insidious force of evil among us, elusive to the average person on the street, with stunning influence on the future of this nation. This cabal of wolves in sheep's clothing acts as false messiahs and delusional imposters who offer irresistible allure to the masses. The unthinkable is happen- ing: the death of freedom in America.

The American way is being threatened as never before. Many perils that are all working together and coming to a head about the same time are overwhelming our nation today. We are confronted by enemies within and without, just like Israel of old. The challenges we face are monumental, complex, unwarranted, universal hostility against our nation. We are engaged in an inescapable, end-time, cosmic struggle between good and evil. Deep in the heart of every American is a sense of bewilderment and loss of control of their immediate future to random forces and factors beyond their control. The middle class is being destroyed. It is unimaginable that 2% owns most of the wealth of the nation.

The American dream is becoming the American nightmare. Needless to say, though all of this is happening, it may appear that America still remains the land of opportunity. The greatest threat to America is diminishing expectations among the middle class. The poor at the bottom of the food chain have long ago given up hope. The nation has become complacent, has lost the American dream and accepted the status quo. The other troubling issue is that people have become so desensitized to moral erosion that nothing now violates our sense of shame. Each one of us needs to understand that this is not the American way. Can you imagine what would happen if we continue on this path?

History has proven to us over and over again that this is a common path to destruction. We are sliding towards a predicament that preceeds the death of civilization and empires. We are living in the most solemn period in human history and America, as a sole superpower, is crumbling. We are our own enemy. We forgot the source of the dream. Ours is a dream anchored in divine providence. It is an impossible dream without God. Our rise and fall is inherent and inactively and inescapably tied to our relationship with God, like Israel of old. Whether we are aware of it or not, God is in control.

If you are like most people, religion has no business in the public square and in business. It is regarded as useless in real life, and it is beyond most people's comfort zone. Most people have been burned out by religion. Regardless of one's upbringing, people are turning away from religion. The problem lies in a "made in America" religion without relationship with Christ: a fast food version of Christianity that sells spiritual junk food.

This kind of religion makes one feel powerless, inadequate and unworthy. This religious indoctrination makes people dislike themselves, which is conducive to depression and compulsive behavior. It is not surprising that most religious people in this country are on prescription drugs. Religion makes people hate themselves "as is" and they want to improve and be better people in vain. People hold on to these false beliefs and false assumptions and, when they fail to live up to their beliefs, they simply reject this unrealistic lifestyle. They go the way of the world and hate religion. This "made in America" Christianity is based upon works of righteousness. It is self-actualization. It is focused on self-improvement. Christian discipleship is nothing but self-discipline or self-realization. Where is God in all this?

The other side of the coin is cheap grace: everything goes, no guilt, no shame, do whatever you want, you are covered, all you have to do is show up on Sunday and pay up. This is "feel good" religion. These religious folks develop high self-esteem. They love their religion.

Both religious experiences are "the opium of the people" and a departure from the religion that made America great. They are both an exercise in futility and irrationality.

True Christianity is Christ calling us to be receivers and not achievers. It is not ability but availability to Christ's grace alone.

America is in trouble because the church has lost the path. There is a need to recalibrate our minds and re-align with God by returning to our old time religion which made America great. Life is a great teacher; we have learned that willpower religion or cheap grace will not save us. There is a point in life when you have to stop and say, "this is not working!" That moment is now!

We should note that, as much as we blame spiritual apostasy for our present dilemma, the other real danger to the future of our nation is an adversarial intelligence embedded in our society: appalling social titans who are opposed particularly to America's providential history. They are committed to de-sanctified politics. The Christian right, unfortunately, has no clear counterattack strategy.

The critical question is, "what can lovers of America do or is it too late?" Time is still on our side as it is never too late with God. However, there is a need for an uprising to take back America.

The first thing to do is to come to terms with the fact that the current financial and social catastrophe we are facing was not shaped by fick- le fate but was created by smart social engineers with a plan. There is currently no real resistance to the path that they have put America on.

The folly of the masses is avoiding and neglecting the details behind the present tragedy to their peril. There is no virtue in remaining ignorant and neutral. The inevitable conclusion is the end of western civilization. We must find the causes of the present dilemma and then take action to reverse its impact. There is a way out.

Chapter Two

THE DILEMMA

As I ref lect upon the imminent future of America, it seems obvious that, unless God intervenes, the current financial, political and social challenges we are facing, if they continue to intensify, will culminate in a complete meltdown. Most people agree that America is on the wrong path but disagree on the solution. The way out is up. We have to look to God who made America great in the first place.

The American people are enchanted with their greatness. Inherent within their culture is the sense of arrogance and pride. This façade of self-importance blocks the soul from reaching out to its God. The problems we are facing are beyond our human capacity. It is time to stop hoping and start the process of moving from crisis to Christ.

The crisis we are facing will not just go away. It is not a matter of chance, but choices that everyone has to make. It is often said that challenges in life do not make you or break you but reveal you. America is being exposed. The question is, "what do we do now?" The future is more important than the past glory.

The task ahead of us is not to reform our nation, but to transform it by the power of God. It is something more profound than a return to past glory: we are going higher. The fact is that we are going through an identity crisis, that we are divided, confused, disillusioned and polarized. We need to stop and re-orient. The America of today is incompatible with the Judeo-Christian values that made America great.

The American religious right is on a collision course with the liberal left. The religious right wants to uphold the Judeo-Christian values and the left wants to remove the moral restraint imposed by the Ten Commandments. There is an all-out attempt to normalize deviant behavior. Hedonism will destroy America. The political topography or landscape reflects the cultural division. If this process continues, it will lead to chaos and social fragmentation. The signs of the forewarnings of the coming social upheaval are everywhere.

There is no doubt that America is facing a massive hidden iceberg ready to sink the nation like the titanic. The insidious forces of darkness are relentlessly wreaking havoc upon this nation. What's happening across America is alarming and maddening. It is an epic battle between the far left and the far right. There are intriguing, colossal plots to cleanse America of its Christian heritage. The stage is being set for the inevitable endgame: the removal of Judeo-Christian values from the public square.

The quietist Christians are largely interested in the rapture and see any effort to restore America as counterproductive to their blessed hope. The apostate church is happy to compromise and co-exist. They are ready to assimilate and follow the way of the world. The true believers in Christ, who live holy lives, will be isolated, rejected and persecuted. They will live in constant turbulence. Dark and sinister forces are formulating a way to single out the rejectionists of the new morality, which is totally opposed to Biblical absolutes, and which labels them haters. They will be forced to compromise and be politically correct.

God is going to respond by sending unusual natural disasters, unprecedented earthquakes, pestilence, torrential rains, hurricanes, tsunami combined with social unrest, economic meltdowns and nuclear holocaust as warnings and judgments on this nation for its rebellion against God. The skeptics will call this a myth based upon Biblical fiction. They will find out when it is too late.

It is my prayer that America will not miss her appointment with God. The present states of America and the world make Biblical prophecy more relevant than ever before. America is on a journey and every journey has an end. This journey will come to a sudden end; many will be caught unprepared to meet their creator.

The rising of America as one nation under God was a watershed in the annals of history. God's plan for America was for her to win nations to Christ. America has lost her call and turned her back on God. She has chosen to go the way of the pagan world. Her judgment is imminent. The scripture says that to him much is given much is expected. America is the epicenter of the coming judgment and Israel ground zero. Can America be saved? It is never too late with God's grace to save the union. The redemption of this nation is conditional upon America giving heed to this warning given in the Holy Scriptures

> *"If My people who are called by My name will humble*
> *themselves, and pray and seek My face, and turn from*
> *their wicked ways, then I will hear from heaven, and*
> *will forgive their sin and heal their land."*
> 2 Chronicles 7:14

God's desire is restoration and reconciliation but we, as his creation, must humble ourselves, pray and turn from our wicked ways. Though, it looks too late as you look into the Eastern sky. The eye of the storm is approaching, it is already gathering strength and in its pathway is destructive rubble being scattered and tens of thousands of lives being lost. The eye of the storm is circling the Middle East and causing a chaotic crescendo. It is crucial to observe that America is caught in the middle of this perfect storm. The underlying cause of the conflict is a looming threat to American interests. There is no doubt that we cannot solve this conflict since the hand of God is being lifted from us. We are like Samson after his hair was cut off: our power is gone. Our influence is a thing of the past; the nations of the world no lon- ger respect us.

The basis of America's Manifest Destiny is in direct correlation with its relationship with God. It's consistent with Israel's ancient history. She was chosen and set apart and she turned her back on God. And so God judged her and scattered her among the nations. This is a precedent to learn from, as there is nothing new under the sun. Theologian Kierkegaurd said: "Life must be lived forward but must only be understood backward."

The only hope is to return to God who enabled America to rise to sole superpower status by His grace. Israel is America's prototype. When she repented, she was saved from her enemies and restored. Our nation today is hated by every nation, bombed by every tragedy, crushed by the heaviest debt as a leading debtor nation in the world, afflicted by international terrorism and battered by every nation in the United Nations.

America is its own enemy; she has moved so deep into the mainstream of paganism and hedonism and is fast losing her manifest destiny and declining into the abyss. The picture in my mind is that of a herd of wildebeests stampeding and racing towards the edge of a cliff and into the abyss, unaware. Mainstream America today has such an impulse towards egotism, materialism and intellectualism and is throwing away its dependence on God. Such a pessimistic argument is difficult to refute, as pride is the celebrated essence of the American way both on Main Street and Wall Street. There is a popular assumption in this country that America is self-made. This ominous mistake is a source of America's downfall. Nations rise and fall by divine decree.

> *"The wicked shall be turned into hell, and all the*
> *nations that forget God." Psalm 9:17*

Contrary to the common assumption that we chart our own future, God is in control of the future.

The critical question is, "will America perish without warning?" God forbid! The real question is, "will the people listen or will it be like in the days of Noah?" It is not coincidence that you are reading this book. Its pages convey the warning from God to His people. Perhaps the American people will not have Israel's mindset to continue in their rebellion. They did and God destroyed them.

We have gone beyond the point of no return. If it were not for the grace of God, we would have already perished. We are living on borrowed time. The fact is that the eye of the perfect storm has already hit the Middle East and is moving towards our shores. The current signs of the time suggest that there is no time to waste. Now is the time to act!

Chapter Three

THE FINAL WARNING

The time of the fulfillment of President Washington's vision at Valley Forge in the bitter winter of 1777 is near. He saw three perils that would come against the Republic. Two of the perils have come and gone, the last, and third one, is upon us. Here is the vision in his own words:

THE FIRST PERIL – THE REVOLUTION

"Presently I hear a voice saying, "*Son of the Republic, look and learn*" while at the same time my visitor extended her arm eastwardly, I now beheld a heave white vapor at some distance rising fold upon fold. This gradually dissipated, and I looked upon a stranger scene. Before me lay spread out in one vast plain all the countries of the world – Europe, Asia, Africa and America. I saw rolling and tossing between Europe and America the billows of the Atlantic, and between Asia and America lay the Pacific.

"*Son of the Republic*", said the same mysterious voice as before. "*Look and learn*". At that moment I beheld a dark, shadowy being, like an angel, standing or rather f loating in mid-air, between Europe and America. Dipping water out of the ocean in the hollow of each hand, he sprinkled some upon America with his right hand, while with his left hand he cast some on Europe. Immediately a cloud raised from these countries, and joined in mid-ocean. For a while it remained stationary, and then moved slowly westward, until it enveloped America in its murky folds. Sharp f lashes of lightning gleamed through it at intervals, and I heard the smothered groans and cries of the American people.

THE SECOND PERI-THE CIVIL WAR

"Second time the angel dipped water from the ocean, and sprinkled it out as before. The dark cloud was then drawn back to the ocean, in whose heaving billows it sank from view a third time I heard the mysterious voice saying, "*Son of the Republic, look and learn*" I cast my eyes upon America and beheld villages and towns and cities springing up one after another until the whole land from the Atlantic to the Pacific was dotted with them.

"Again, I heard the mysterious voice say, "*Son of the republic, the end of the century cometh look and learn*". At this the dark shadowy angel turned his face southward, and from Africa I saw an ill omened spec- ter approach our land. It f littered slowly over every town and city of the latter. The inhabitants presently set themselves in battle array against each other. As I continued looking I saw a bright angel, on whose brow rested a crown of light, on which was traced the word "union", bearing the American f lag which he placed between the divided nation, an said, "Remember ye are brethren". Instantly, the inhabitants, casting from them their weapons became friends once more, and united around the National Standard.

THE THIRD PERIL – AMERICA'S JUDGMENT?

"And again I heard the mysterious voice saying "*Son of the Republic, look and learn*". At this the dark shadowy angel placed a trumpet to his mount, and blew three distinct blasts and taking water from the ocean, he sprinkled it upon Europe, Asia and Africa. Then my eyes beheld a fearful scene: From each of these countries arose thick, black clouds that were soon joined into one. Throughout this mass there gleamed a dark red light by which I saw hordes of armed men, who, moving with the cloud, marched by land and sailed by sea to Amer- ica. Our country was enveloped in this volume of cloud, and I saw these vast armies devastate the whole country and burn the villages, towns and cities that I beheld springing up. As my ears listened to the thundering of the cannon, clashing of sword, and the shouts and cries of millions in mortal combat. I heard again the mysterious voice say- ing, "*Son of the Republic, look and learn*". When the voice had ceased, the dark shadow angel placed his trumpet once more to his mouth, and blew a long and fearful blast.

"Instantly a light as of a thousand suns shone down from above me, and pierced and broke into fragments the dark cloud which enveloped America. At the same moment the angel upon whose head still shone the word Union, and who bore our national f lag in one hand and a sword in the other, descended from the heavens attended by legions of white spirits. These immediately joined the inhabitants of America, who I perceived were will nigh overcome, but who immediately taking courage again, closed up their broken ranks and renewed the battle.

"Again amid the fearful noise of the conflict, I heard the mysterious voice saying, "*Son of the Republic, look and learn*". As the voice ceased, the shadowy angel for the last time dipped water from the ocean and sprinkled it upon America. Instantly the dark cloud rolled back, together with the armies it had brought, leaving the inhabitants of the land victorious!

"Then once more I beheld the villages, towns and cities springing up where I had seen them before, while the bright angel, planting the azure standard he Had brought in the midst of them, cried with a loud voice: "*While the stars remain, and the heavens send down dew upon the earth, so long shall the Union last*". And taking from his brow the crown on which blazoned the word "*Union*", he placed it upon the Standard while the people, kneeling down, said, "*Amen*".

"The scene instantly began to fade and dissolve, and I at last saw nothing but the rising, curling vapor I at first beheld. This also disappearing, I found myself once more gazing upon the mysterious visitor, who, in the same voice I had heard before said, "*Son of the Republic, what you have seen is thus interpreted: Three great perils will come upon the Republic. The most fearful is the third, but in this greatest conflict the whole world united shall not prevail against her. Let every child of the Republic learn to live for his God, his land and the Union*", With these words the vision vanished, and I started from my seat and felt that I had seen a vision wherein had been shown to me the birth, progress, and destiny of the United States."

This ended General George Washington's vision and prophecy for the United States of America as told in his words.

Chapter Four

THE LOS LUNAS DECALOGUE STONE

Here lies the matrix of America's Manifest Destiny, the secret ancient Deuteronomic code that constitutes the mystery of America's indivisibility, the Los Lunas Decalogue Stone and the Tetragrammaton (the four Hebrew consonant letters that translate into the name of the God of Abraham, commonly rendered as Yahweh).

The Decalogue, or Ten Commandments Inscription, is carved in old Hebrew letters. The letters are almost identical in shape and font-style to the Paleo-Hebrew that was used during the Solomonic era. The Hebrew writing style changed after Babylonian exile 536 B.C. The Los Lunas Decalogue Inscription is 3000 years old and was written about 1000B.C.

The boulder with the old Hebrew inscription is estimated to weigh 80-100 tons and was found in the Hidden Mountain, in New Mexico, 35 miles south of Albuquerque. It is now tilted by approximately 40 degrees, indicating that over the centuries it moved 2/3 of the dis- tance from the Mesa top to the valley f loor since it broke off. Each line of the message is to be read from right to left. Each statement is separated from the next one by a dot sign which was typical of the Paleo-Hebrew Inscriptions. A good example of this is found in the Moabite Stone of the same period.

Here is the detailed, interlinear translation of the ancient Los Lunas Decalogue Inscription in modern- day English:

"I am Jehovah your God who has taken you out of the land of Egypt, from the house of slavery. There must be no other gods before my face. You must not make any idol. You must not take the name of Jehovah in vain. Remember the Sabbath day and keep it holy. Honor your father and your mother so that your days may be long in the land that Jehovah your God has given to you. You must not murder. You must not commit adultery. You must not steal. You must not give a false witness against your neighbor. You must not desire the wife of your neighbor nor anything that is his."

Professor Robert H. Pfeiffer of Harvard University made the first translations of this ancient Palio Hebrew inscription. The local Indians called the Hidden Mountain "Mystery's Mountain" because of the inscriptions that they couldn't read. Many other modern scholars all agree that the Los Lunas Inscription is a Deuteronomic version of the Sinai Ten Commandments given to Moses by God. Among them are such men as Professor James D. Taboor, of the Department of Religious Studies, University of North Carolina and Professor Frank Hibben, local historian and archaeologist from the University of New Mexico. They are convinced that the inscription is ancient and that the inscription is authentic. Dr. Cyrus Goren, a historian of ancient Near East civilization, promoted the idea that Near Eastern voyagers visited the new world centuries ago. Stan Fox,

a linguist and Bible expert from Colchester England, translated the Los Lunas Inscription and confirmed it was an ancient inscription of the Ten Commandments.

The age of the Los Lunas Inscription is resolved by comparing the Los Lunas Inscription to other Phoenician and Paleo-Hebrew inscription samples from the Mediterranean Middle East of that period. The Los Lunas Inscription was written in old Hebrew and Phoenician charac- ters used identically during 1100 to 600 B.C.E. After the Babylonian exile, old Hebrew was replaced with the square-Hebrew alphabet.

The question is, "Why were the ten commandments chiseled into the rock 3000 years ago in America and the Tetragrammaton secret name of God?"

Does America share the same calling to be the people of God like Israel? Is there a precedent of the Decalogue Inscription in the mountains in Israel? What did it mean? Where is it? The answer can only be found in the Holy Scriptures of the Hebrews.

God told Moses to tell the children of Israel to write the Decalogue upon great stones on Mount Ebal, upon entering the land.

> *And Moses with the elders of Israel commanded the people, saying, Keep all the commandments which I command you this day. And it shall be on the day when ye shall pass over Jordan unto the land which the Lord thy God giveth thee, that thou shalt set thee up great stones, and plaister them with plaister: And thou shalt write upon them all the words of this law, when thou art passed over, that thou mayest go in unto the land which the Lord thy God giveth thee, a land that floweth with milk and honey: as the Lord God of thy fathers hath promised thee. Therefore it shall be when ye be gone over Jordan, that ye shall set up these stones, which I command you this day, in mount Ebal, and thou shalt plaster them with plaister. And there shalt thou build an altar unto the Lord thy God, and altar of stones: thou shalt not lift up any iron tool upon them. Thou shalt build the altar of the Lord thy God of whole stones: and thou shalt offer burnt offerings thereon unto the Lord thy God: And thou shalt offer peace offerings, and shalt eat there, and rejoice before the Lord thy God. And thou shalt write upon the stones all the words of this law very plainly. (1)*

Mount Ebal is adjacent to Mount Gerizim. It is the higher of the two. It is 3077 feet above sea level and the valley provides a natural amphitheater with wonderful acoustic properties for a large gathering. Joshua obeyed God and built the altar and wrote the Decalogue on the great stones. A couple of years ago I picked up a stone from the altar, which I keep in my office.

Over three thousand years ago, at Mount Ebal, Joshua, at the end of his life, gathered the children of Israel to renew the covenant. It is here that he declared:

> *And it shall come to pass, if thou shalt hearken diligently unto the voice of the Lord they God, to observe and to do all his commandments which I command thee this day, that the Lord they God will set thee on high above all nations of the earth. And all these blessings shall come on thee, and overtake thee, if thou shalt hearken to the voice of the Lord thy God. Blessed shalt thou be in the city, and blessed shalt thou be in the field. Blessed shall be the fruit of thy body, and the fruit of thy ground, and the fruit of thy cattle, and increase of thy kine, and the flocks of thy sheep. Blessed shall be the basket and thy store. Blessed shalt thou be when thou comest in, and blessed shalt thou be when thou goest out. The Lord shall cause thine enemies that rise up against thee to be smitten before they face; they shall come out against thee one way, and flee before thee seven ways. The Lord shall command the blessing upon thee one- way, and flee before thee seen ways. The Lord shall command the blessing upon thee in thy storehouses, and in all that thou settest thine hand unto; and he shall bless thee in the land which the Lord thy God giveth thee. The Lord shall establish thee an holy people unto himself, as he hath sworn unto thee, if thou shalt keep the commandments of the Lord thy God, and walk in his ways. And all people of the earth shall see that thou art called by the name of the Lord; and they shall be afraid of thee. And the Lord shall make thee plenteous in goods, in*

> *the fruit of they body, and in the fruit of thy cattle, and in*
> *the fruit of thy ground, in the land which the Lord sware*
> *unto thy fathers to give thee. The Lord shall open unto*
> *thee his good treasure, the heaven to give the rain unto thy*
> *land in his season, and to bless all the work of thine hand:*
> *and thou shalt lend unto many nations, and thou shalt not*
> *borrow. And the Lord shall make thee the head, and not*
> *the tail; and thou shalt be above only, and thou shalt not*
> *be beneath; if that thou hearken unto the commandments*
> *of the Lord thy God, which I command thee this day, to*
> *observe and to do them. (2)*

If you want to read the whole declaration, you can find it in the book of Deuteronomy, chapter 28 in the Holy Bible.

The Decalogue Inscriptions on Mount Ebal represent divine sover- eignty over the land, a territorial sphere whose constitution is the Ten Commandments. This theocratic people would serve the Lord as a chosen people and, if they disobeyed, they would be judged severely. God promised to perpetuate His covenant blessings for a thousand generations towards those who love Him. The covenant way of life was divinely dictated in the Ten Commandments as a standard of his people's consecration and dedication to Him.

The Mount Ebal Decalogue Inscription was a divine declaration of His protection over the land, a sign of divine election, a symbol of indivisibility and divine favor. It explained their peculiarity as the most blessed people on earth. The finger of God Almighty wrote the Ten Commandments, the most sacred writing on earth. God confirmed his election of Israel by having his law written on Mount Ebal. The blessings from obedience and the curses from disobedience were proclaimed from Mount Ebal. There are only two mountains, Mount Ebal in Israel and Hidden Mountain, New Mexico USA, where these covenant blessing were written on the mountains three thousand years ago. America and Israel share a common destiny.

The Los Lunas Decalogue and Tetragrammaton, composed of four Hebrew consonants with letters that spell Yahweh the name of the God of Abraham, the Holy One of Israel, Yahweh, were written in the Mystery Mountains of New Mexico identical to Mount Ebal Decalogue Inscription, a sign and proclamation of the sovereignty of Gods law over America. America is a chosen people, blessed for obedience to God or cursed for disobedience.

As the Mount Ebal Decalogue Inscription was across the river Jordan so is the Los Lunas site itself. It used to be accessible via Rio Puerco, a contributory to the Rio Grande, which in turn leads to the Gulf of Mexico. Archaeologist Ellsworth Huntington said that the area used to be f looded during the first millennium B.C. which would have allowed easy navigation along the Rio Grande and Rio Puerco for boats coming from the Gulf of Mexico. The ocean going f leets of King Solomon and Hiram went up the Rio Grande to New Mexican trading outposts at "Mystery Mountain", an ancient Holy Jewish settlement in the New World during the bronze era. The sacred ancient literature bears record of such ancient voyages.

> *For the king (Solomon) had at sea a navy of Tharshish*
> *with the navy of Hiram: once in three years came the*
> *navy of Tharshish, bringing gold, and silver, ivory, and*
> *apes, and peacocks. (3)*
>
> *And Hiram sent in the navy his servants, shipmen that had*
> *knowledge of the sea, with the servants of Solomon. (4)*

We know that the voyages they undertook in their joint f leets took three years to complete. The reasonable explanation for such long travelling periods seems to be the fact that they had trans-Atlantic trade outposts, in the New World at the Los Lunas site in New Mexico, USA.

The Native American Indians in New Mexico never developed a character-based alphabet. The Los Lunas Inscription, done in old Hebrew, is a genuine chronicle of an incredible moment from actual events in the ancient history of America that extended the Abrahamic covenant blessing to this nation. The Los Lunas Decalogue Inscription is located on New Mexico State Trust Land and is classified as "Mystery Stone."

There is an unidentified petroglyph depicting a face with what looks like a crown on its head. It is less than 50 yards away from the Decalogue Inscription. Crowns were unknown to American Indians. They are of Middle Eastern Mediterranean origin. This may indicate a visit by high-ranking Mediterranean royalty, wearing a crown. The survey of the whole site shows the existence of some leftovers of an ancient fortification, most likely a Jewish trade outpost during the Solomonic era.

The only possible way to find the answer to this question of "who is this Mediterranean King that visited Los Lunas site three thousand years ago?" is to go to ancient records. We know, from Biblical records of the time, that the Phoenician King Hiram's seamen had knowledge of Trans-oceanic trade missions and that they worked together with King Solomon's seamen. Hiram could be the Mediterranean King that visited the New World. The chance of King Hiram visiting a Jewish sacred site at Los Lumas site is very slim because of Jewish religious laws that forbid Gentiles from such holy sites. This was a sacred site similar to the Mount Ebal Decalogue Inscription site, with an altar and the Tetragrammaton name of God, Yahweh. The most compelling probability is King Solomon. He would be welcome to visit such a sacred site in Judaism. He would have traveled to Los Lu- nas for a royal visit to extend his sovereignty and annex the land, as ancient Kings often did after they conquered the territory, to collect the spoil and to give stipulations to the vassal state. Though the Bible is silent and extra biblical records have not yet been uncovered at the site, one thing we know for sure, royalty from the Mediterranean visited this Jewish Holy site during the bronze era. According to Jew- ish religious traditions, it could not be some one other than a Jewish King. The most persuasive and predominant likelihood is King Sol- omon. He was the wisest man and the most blessed Mediterranean Royalty with a trans-oceanic f leet recorded in scriptures. He had the financial resources to undertake such a voyage and royal mission to the new World.

There is a Biblical precedent when Joshua conquered the land. He gathered the people back to the Mount Ebal Decalogue Inscription site as head of the nation. They had completed the conquest of the land and were enjoying the covenant blessing of God when he gathered the people back to the Mount Ebal Decalogue Inscription site. This was a solemn assembly with their leader to renew their covenant commitment. The Los Lunas Decalogue Inscription site was the most sacred place in the New World for Jewish royalty to pronounce the Abrahamic blessings upon his economic and political sphere of influence in the New World and to extend his sovereignty over the land.

The ancient matrix, the Deuteronomic code, the covenant, evidenced in the Los Lunas Decalogue Inscription, in New Mexico, written three thousand years ago by the Hebrews, defines, over providential indivisibility, our spiritual ethos, our orientation towards justice for all, our consistent passion for liberty and our optimism. All of these constitute the dynamics of the ancient matrix consistently peculiar and unique to America. The envisaged trajectory of the ancient path- way, predetermined by God for this nation, is being worked out in our history today. This ancient Hebrew dichotomy galvanizes our spirits to predominantly pursue freedom for the oppressed in our world. This inherited manifest destiny perpetuates our high self-esteem and our deep-seated belief that God is on our side. Our self-consciousness is intrinsically defined by our divine endowment superimposed by God's ancient covenant extended to this land by the Hebrews three thousand years ago during the bronze era.

Chapter Five

THE SOLOMONIC GLOBAL EXPLORATION

The American dream—what is it? The task of understanding this amazing triumphant saga, the drama and charm of this historical tapestry, which defines the American ethos was conceived by the founding fathers, 240 years ago, as one of life, liberty and the pursuit of happiness.

Nowhere has been such a compelling, timeless dream realized. Subsequent history bears witness that it has become a paradigm destined to inspire the oppressed masses for generations to come. Notwithstanding the fact that today America stands tall among the community of nations as rich, beautiful, magnificent, prosperous, prestigious, indivisible, exuberant and endowed with the highest standard of living in the world. These perennial, vivacious sentiments,

gathered together, constitute and attribute to a character independently and distinctively American. It's military and economic dynamism and self-image impels her to assume a dominant and preeminent role in global policing. She is a beacon of hope in the global village.

The rest of the world is intrigued, mystified, frightened, outraged, stirred up and perplexed about America's f lamboyant pomposity and its frontier attitude of indivisibility and an ingrained sense of superiority.

The shift of the balance of power from the Old World in a relatively short time to America has become a locus of intense controversy and debate.

How such a nation, relatively young, can rise to stardom as the sole superpower in the world? The matrix is hidden in ages past in the ancient Hebrew literature;

> *"That which is has already been; and what is to be has already been." Ecclesiastes 3:15*

Strange as it may seem, America's predominance and its emergence to the pinnacle of power constitute a convergence of pathways that go back to Solomon's Temple in Jerusalem 3000 years ago, on Mt. Moriah. America secured a place of privilege and blessing endowed upon every people that blesses Abraham's seed as promised in the sacred and ancient scriptures.

> *"I will bless those who bless you. And whoever curses you I will curse: and all peoples on earth will be blessed through you." Genesis 12:3*

This divine immutable commitment of God explains the mystifying matrix of American greatness. The lineal descendants of Abraham are the carriers of the covenant blessings to the nations. Through the ages, they have been battered by every tempest, aff licted by every ordeal, crushed by every weight, bombarded by every tragedy, hated by every nation yet they remain the dispenser of the divine blessing to all the peoples of the earth as God promised.

The Bible is the bridge between ancient Israel and modern America. This view may seem unwarranted, until you look at the obvious Hebraic influence upon the essential characteristics that constitute our nation. Ancient Israel, strange as it may seem, is a prototype of modern day America. The Bible shaped America's self-consciousness. Its early history was molded by Judeo Christian ethics. This Biblical orientation towards a conception of a unique self-image and consis- tent distinction is derived from its continual providential interven- tion in its history. There are amazing similarities between ancient Israel and America.

The big question that confronts us at this critical juncture in our history is whether there is a common denominator between Israel's golden age and America today. This question is indispensable to those seeking to understand America's dilemma for eradicating its spirituality. The Solomonic era was identical to modern day America, Israel was a prosperous and prestigious global superpower yet, when she forgot God, she was destroyed. Will history repeat itself? Will our bogus values of consumerism and materialism prevail over the epidemic social ills that destroyed Israel as a superpower in ancient times? It is not surprising that there is an incredible indication that America was part of the Solomonic sphere of influence. He extended the Abrahamic covenant blessings to this country. America is a recipient of the ancient providence of God. These historical precedents, dating back to the Solomonic era, lay the foundation for America's prophetic destiny. The fact that Solomonic trans-oceanic voyages to the New World to gather gold for the temple of God came here brings us to the Biblical conclusion that America has a divine manifest destiny.

America is an amazing repository of extra-Biblical inscriptions dat- ing back to Solomon's age that confirms Semitic and Punic voyages to the New World. Incredible inscriptions have been found all over North America and kept at Harvard University and elsewhere. Re- cently, Harvard Professor Barry Fell deciphered most of them and authenticated them as genuine.

According to Professor Barry Fell's book, America BC, there are hundreds of inscriptions among such places as New Hampshire, Vermont, Tennessee, California, Oklahoma, New England, New York, Rhode Island, Maine and many other places. Until the present day, however, Western xenophobia marginalized these enormous historical facts though inherent in these antiquities are America's manifest destiny. This is a Biblical phenomenon in which God tells the end from the beginning.

These discoveries created a dialectical crisis for colonial imperialism. The politically correct thing was to reject them as forgeries because they were viewed as abstractions from the church's mission to evangelize the pagans. The Old World had no interest in intellectualizing the public perception of its overseas natives but to emotionalize the Western church to evangelize the lost heathens in the lost continent.

Professor Barry Fell's book shatters preconceived ideas about the Americas during the Bronze era. It ardently, eloquently, meticulously documents incisive, thought-provoking translations of ancient inscriptions found all over the New World. He traces the history of some of the indigenous peoples in the Americas to the descendants of the Phoenicians, Hebrews, North Africans, and European Celts of Southern Spain.

The translations of these historical chronicles are as radical a departure from the norm as Copernicus's revelation during the dark ages, when He argued against the accepted Orthodoxy promulgated by Claudius Ptolemy in Alexandria around 150 AD that the earth was fixed at the center of the universe.

Copernicus's hypothesis of a heliocentric (sun-centered) planetary system was considered too revolutionary and was rejected by the academia of his day, which were later proven wrong. Professor Berry Fell's findings are disputed, disregarded, disrespected, discarded and contested as problematic and controversial because they conflict with the stereotype assumptions sanctioned by the establishment. These extra-Biblical inscriptions confirm the Biblical records of the Solomonic global trans-oceanic trade missions in 1000 BC.

It is not coincidental that the colonial imperial powers ignored those ancient artifacts because the heathens were castigated, vilified and dehumanized. Thus, for instance, if these tribes were lost Teutonic and Semitic races from the Old World, it would immediately change the notion of racial superiority. Anthropology defined status in those days. The degradation of the heathens was absolute and absurd.

These ancient inscriptions were regarded as plow markers, meaningless and useless, because Indians were regarded as people without a past. Today, 500 years after Columbus, Harvard Prof. Barry Fell has deciphered most of these inscriptions to confirm that this is indeed true of some of the natives or first Americans. It is an undeniable fact that most of them came from Asia across the Bering Sea to the Americas.

THE MATRIX OF AMERICAS MANIFEST DESTINY REVEALED

Its not surprising that these ancient inscriptions were suppressed and denied for many years because they created a perplexing conundrum to the whole rationale for global colonialism, especially in a world framed by western imperialism. By trivializing and denying these ancient records, America was denied her place in the Abrahamic sphere of covenant blessings extended to her by the Solomonic trans-Atlantic trade posts in the New World, 3000 years ago.

In 1838, an Iberian inscription identical to the ancient Phoenician (Punic) was found at Grave Creek in West Virginia. Prof. Copenhaven recognized it as written in a form of first millennium Punic alphabet. An English epigrapher, D. Divinger, confirmed that the language was basic Semitic and that all the words are found in the modern day Semitic Standard dictionaries.

God promised Israel that wherever they go, He will extend His cove- nantal sphere of blessings and manifest destiny over those lands. This is what He promised in the sacred scriptures.

> *"I will give you every place where you set your foot, as I promised Moses." Joshua 1:3*

America is a sphere of Abrahamic blessing dating back to the time of King Solomon because of these ancient voyages to the New World. The contribution of the gold from the New World in the building of the Temple of the Holy One of Israel on Mount Moriah primarily secured for future generation's divine destiny being played out in history today. America is beautiful because God is a covenant-keeping God.

In 1889, the Smithsonian Institution found an ancient mould near Little Tennessee River—nine skeletons and a curious inscription and a pair of brass bracelets. The stone is known as the Bat Creek Inscription and has characters scratched across its surface. In 1960, the inscription was found to resemble the ancient script of the Phoenicians which relates both to Cananite and Hebrew scripts. It is closely similar to ancient Paleo-Hebrew. A Hebrew scholar, Syrups Gordon, translated several of the characters on the inscription to read for the Judeans.

THE BIBLE CONFIRMS THE AUTHENTICITY OF THE ANCIENT INSCRIPTIONS

The inerrant and infallible Biblical literature confirms the existence of a Judean ocean-going f leet during the Solomonic time.

> *"The King had a f leet of trading ships at sea along with the ships of Hiram. Once every three years it returned carrying gold, silver and ivory, and apes and baboons. King Solomon was greater in riches and wisdom than all the other kings of the earth."*
> *1 Kings 10:22-23*

The Solomonic Kingdom was a small people with a large place in history. His people traced their origin from the migration into Canaan from Ur between the Tigris and the Euphrates River of their ancestor Abraham, a friend of God. Solomon transformed a tribal league into unparalleled global economic power with trans-oceanic trade posts in the New World three thousand years ago.

Solomon established an economic alliance with the Phoenician King Hiram to achieve his global trade objectives. Solomon built a port and a trans-oceanic f leet at Zion Geber on the Gulf of Aqaba and from there he conducted global trade in precious metals. This was a 'golden age' for Israel. They were a superpower of the day. God was with them. It is not surprising that Solomon, as the wisest man that ever lived on earth, would explore the world. Unquestionably this was a rich and powerful epoch in the history of Israel and global exploration.

Solomon changed the ancient world. He set the world on its way to become what it is today.

> *"God gave Solomon wisdom and very great insight, and*
> *a breadth of understanding as measureless as the sand*
> *on the seashore. Solomon's wisdom was greater than the*
> *wisdom of all the men of the East, and greater than all*
> *the wisdom of Egypt. He was wiser than any other man,*
> *including Ethan the Ezrahite – wiser than Heman.*
> *Calcol and Darda, the sons of Mahol. And his fame*
> *spread to all the surrounding nations. He spoke three*
> *thousand proverbs and his songs numbered a thousand*
> *and five. He described plant life, from the cedar of*
> *Lebanon to the hyssop that grows out of walls. He also*
> *taught about animals and birds, reptiles and fish. Men of*
> *all nations came to listen to Solomon's wisdom, sent by all*
> *the kings of the world, who had heard of his wisdom."*
> *1 Kings 4:29-34*

The Hebrews knew that the world was round hundreds of years before Martin Behaim made the first terrestrial globe in Nuremberg, Germany in 1492. The Hebrew Holy Scriptures revealed that to them while the rest of the world was still in the stone age. Isaiah wrote hundreds of years before Christ about it.

> *"God sits enthroned above the circle of the earth, and its*
> *people are like grasshoppers, He stretches out the heavens*
> *like a canopy, and spread them out like a tent to live*
> *in." Isaiah 40:22*

It is apparent that God entrusted to the Hebrews this information and they utilized it by establishing global trade. Surprisingly, many in this space-age doubt that these ancient people would have known what the rest of mankind just discovered as recently as five hundred years ago. One has to bear in mind that divine revelation, and not rationality, revealed these things to them.

Biblical literature destroys all of our old pre-conceptions and challenges our assumptions and common hallucinations that contribute to our false sense of importance and pride as wiser and smarter than all the past generations. We need to heed the words of the wisest man: "That which is has already been." There is no question that the Jews were not smarter than the rest of mankind. It is obvious that the fundamental reasons for such a quantum leap for the lineal descendants of Israel was the God factor. He told them. He led them. He blessed them. He instructed them. He showed them. He invited them to ask Him whenever they needed guidance.

DAVID SPEAKS OF SUN ROTATION 3000 YEARS AGO

King David said, "the sun travels in his circuit into the end of it (heaven)" (Psalms 19:4-6). Down through the ages, critics denounced the statement as false, until Hubble Telescope verified that the sun actually travels in a circuit covering an enormous orbit that takes two hundred and sixty million years to complete.

BIBLE REVEALS THE HOLE IN SPACE

Job reported more than 3000 years ago that "He stretched out the north over empty space" (Job 26:7). Mitchell Waldrop recently wrote in a science magazine that there is a hole in space – a 300 million light-year gap in the distribution of galaxies in the Northern Hemi-sphere–lying in the general direction of the constellation Bootes. This relative emptiness in the direction of the North of our solar system is not visible to the naked eye. It is only recently, as a result of very careful observation by very powerful telescopes, that scientists have proven that Job was correct.

ANCIENT MANUSCRIPTS REVEAL SEVEN STARS IN THE PLEIADES

Amos said, "Seek him that maketh the seven stars and Orion" (Amos 5:8–King James translation). He was referring to the constellation Pleiades. Again, the critics denounced the Bible because they could not see the seventh star. Now, with powerful telescopes, the seventh star has been confirmed.

ANCIENTS HAD GLOBAL WEATHER PATTERN KNOWLEDGE

Here is another statement that critics again denounced: "All the rivers ran into the sea, yet the sea is not full; to the place from which rivers come (sea) there they return." (Ecclesiastes 1:7) People believed that most rain comes from evaporation from rivers and lakes. The United States Department of Agriculture recently confirmed that most of the water comes from evaporation from the ocean that covers two thirds of the planet's surface. The ancient people of Israel understood the hydrological cycle of evaporation, cloud formation, precipitation and rain with amazing scientific accuracy.

THE ANCIENTS KNEW THE DIAMETER OF THE EARTH AND THE DISTANCES OF THE SUN AND MOON

The Jews spread this knowledge throughout the Mediterranean world. Eratosthenes (276-195 BC) was able to measure the diameter of the earth, which he confirmed was round, by measuring the angle of the sunlight in two Egyptian cities on the same day, with surpris- ing accuracy.

Aristarchus (310-230) measured the position of the moon at different phases to estimate using geometry that the sun is twenty times fur- ther from the earth than the moon.

The knowledge of the ancient people of God continues to confound the skeptics. The Bible is infallible. There is impeccable, solid evidence that God gave them incredible scientific data that modern science is just investigating. To their utter amazement, every Biblical statement that they thought was false is overwhelmingly irrefutable. King Solomon was armed with advanced and incredible God-given scientific knowledge. The Solomonic kingdom was not some Iron Age primitive sphere of influence. He had global economic interests supported by sound scientific knowledge for global exploration.

THE ANCIENT INFORMATION SUPER HIGHWAY TO HEAVEN

Do you know that the Hebrews had access to infinite knowledge through a mystical dial-up connectivity to heaven, allowing them to obtain divine wisdom on any matter, anytime? Moses received the Urim and Thummim from God and, before he died, he told them to put it in the breastplate of the High Priest for safekeeping.

> *"Also put the Urim and the Thummim in the breast plate, so they may be over Aaron's heart whenever he enters the presence of the Lord. Thus Aaron will always bear the means of making decisions for the Israelites over his heart before the Lord."*
> *Exodus 28:30*
>
> *"He placed the breastpiece on him and put the Urim and Thummim in the breastpiece" Leviticus 8:8*
>
> *"He is to stand before Eleazar the priest, who will obtain decisions for him by inquiring of the Urim before the Lord. At his command he and the entire community of the Israelites will go out, and at his command they will come in." Numbers 27:21*

We know that during the reign of King David and Solomon 3000 years ago the Urim and Thummim were still with men. They dialed-up for information whenever they had a crisis or needed immediate guidance and answers.

Our search engines are limited compared to the ancient Hebrew's Urim and Thummim. They knew more than we will ever know. This is why the Judeans had been to Little Tennessee thousands of years before Columbus's voyage. They claimed the New World for the King of Glory on Mt. Zion. The pilgrims, like ancient Jews, were liberated from the tyranny of the apostatized church in Europe and were led to the New World to reclaim the lost continent for the Holy One of Israel. This was in fulfillment of scriptures that clearly tell us "that which is has already been, and what is to be has already been."

Calendar Stile found an inscription in 1874 at Mound in Iowa written in three languages: Egyptian hieroglyphs, Iberian-Punic and Coptic–Libyan. It is in the Putman Museum's repository in Iowa today.

Solomon's divine mandate to build a dwelling place for God on Mount Moriah transformed the ancient world. He mobilized the world for this most sacred task to gather the gold for the Temple of God. He organized trans-oceanic missions to distant countries to bring fine gold to Mount Moriah. He established colonies in overseas places for exploration and exploitation of precious metals for the temple of the Holy One of Israel.

> *"Solomon also made all the furnishings that were in the Lord's temple: the golden altar; the golden table on which was the bread of the Presence; the lampstands of pure gold (five on the right and five on the left, in front of the inner sanctuary); the gold floral work and lamps and tongs; the pure gold basins, wick trimmers, sprinkling bowls, dishes and censers; and the gold sockets for the doors of the innermost room, the Most Holy Place, and also for the doors of the main hall of the temple."*
> *1 Kings 7:48-50*

Is it amazing that America was a melting pot 3000 years ago, peopled by every race, Semitic, Japhetic and Hamitic. All the children of Noah met in America to serve the Holy One of Israel–to build Him a House on earth. The only building designed in heaven and built on earth by mankind. David received the blueprint directly from God.

> *"Then David gave his son Solomon the plans for the portico of the temple, its buildings, its storerooms, its upper parts, its inner rooms and the place of atonement. He gave him the plans of all that the Spirit had put in his mind for the courts of the temple of the Lord and all the surrounding rooms, for the treasuries of the temple of God and for the treasuries for the dedicated things. All this, David said,* **"I have in writing from the hand of the Lord upon me, and he gave me understanding in all the details of the plan."***
> 1 Chronicles 28: 11-12 & 19*

Solomon summoned all of mankind to gather the materials to build this Holy Temple. They sailed together to the ends of the world. They lived together, worked together, played together, prayed together and were blessed together. America today is a recurrent phenomenon of the Solomonic golden age of exploration and global influence.

American gold was used to build Solomon's temple in Jerusalem. This historical precedent suggests the most obvious conclusion that Amer- ica has always had an enormous place in the destiny of mankind. The Bat Creek inscription gives us particularly crucial evidence that America is chosen to play a major part in God's plan of the ages. It is scarcely conceivable that it was coincidental that the Judeans came to America to take gold to Jerusalem to build the Temple without divine guidance. It was a precedent of our relationship with Israel today.

THE HEAVENLY STRUCTURE ON EARTH

Josephus provides detailed eyewitness description of the temple. Also the tannaitic and mishnaic literature gives vivid descriptions. The temple was the most magnificent building in the ancient world, 180 feet long, 90 feet wide and 50 feet high. Solomon spared no expense. He ordered vast quantities of cedar wood from Hiram, King of Tyre. He overlaid the wood with gold from America and around the world. The splendor of Solomon's Temple was magnificent not only in its tremendous size and sumptuous ornamentation but in the amount of fine gold used in its finish.

The temple was built after the heavenly prototype. David received the blueprint from God. Solomon's temple was divided into Ulam (court of Gentiles), the Hekhal (Holy place), Devir (Holy of Holies), the additional structure (yatzia), and the temple treasury. The temple mount enclosure was 144,000 square meters (36 acres) and was the most sacred compound in antiquity. The temple was the axis mundi– the gateway to heaven. The glory of God filled the Solomonic temple. This was the most extraordinary manifestation of Gods presence on earth. Can you imagine that the gold that adorned the holy of holies, the abode of the glory of God on earth came from the New World? What a privilege! Amazing call! Glorious predestination!

The Bat Creek inscription constituted a monumental and undeniable historical connection between ancient Israel and North America. This historical linkage in antiquity was a paradigm of our present day calling. It was the pattern of today as America once again stands together with Israel. This ancient relationship superimposes a hereditary orientation towards present continuation of the manifest destiny of divine providence and election of this nation. Its not surprising that the Puritans rightly believed that America's destiny was prefigured in ancient Israel.

In 1673 Urian Oaks, then President of Harvard, said:

> *"If we lay all things together this commonwealth*
> *seems to exhibit to us specimen or a little model of the*
> *Kingdom of Christ on earth"*

Almost all early Colonialists believed that America was a continuation of Israel's covenant relationship with God. This view is warranted by the fact that historical precedents establish God's will. The ways of God are established of old, He tells us the end from the beginning.

> *"I make known the end from the beginning, from*
> *ancient times, what is still to come, I say: My purpose*
> *will stand, and I will do all that I please."*
> *Isaiah 46:10*

Chapter Six

THE ABRAHAMIC COVENANT BLESSINGS EXTENDED TO AMERICA

Historically, the fact that the first maps that the Italian, Portuguese and Spanish explorers used were made by the Judeans indicates and further confirms that the knowledge of world geography was preserved among the Jewish people for centuries. The first treatise of the Astrolabe device used for calculating the position of heavenly bodies and the position of the ship relative to the stars in the sky was written by a Jew known as Mashallah of Barsa around 800 AD.

When Vasco da Gama set sail from Lisbon for India via Cape of Good Hope in 1497, his ships were outfitted with astrolabes newly perfected by another Jewish astronomer, Abraham ben Samuel Zacuto.

It is believed that Christopher Columbus was a Catholic of Jewish descent. That is why it is not surprising that he entrusted his legacy to the keeper of the gate of Jerusalem. He is listed in the who's who in the Jewish history.

The crucial question is whether the continuum of Jewish connectivity from ancient times with America was not simply coincidental. It is apparently the case, when you realize the fact that the first man to set foot into the New World was a Jew. This is not surprising. According to Christopher Columbus's diary, the first person ashore was one Conversgo Luis de Torres on November 2,

1492. Here is what he wrote about the advent of the first white man in the New World:

> *"The Admiral decided upon sending two Spaniards*
> *one named Rodrigo de Jerez, who lived in Ayamonte*
> *and the other Luis de Torres who had served in the*
> *household of Adelantado of Murcia, and had been a*
> *Jew, knowing Hebrew, Chaldee and some Arabic."*

In accordance with Gods ancient covenant by virtue of Luis de Torris's act as the first Jewish man to step foot on to the New Land, he automatically claimed the New World for the Holy one of Israel as God promised to the Israelites in the book of Joshua:

> *"I will give you every place where you set your foot, as I*
> *promised Moses." Joshua 1:3*

Eventually, Torres was among the first white men to settle in the West Indies as a land baron and lived most of his life on royal pensions in the New World, thereby actualizing and fulfilling the conditions for right of ownership according to the ancient sacred covenant.

The reason that we explore these fundamental precedents, which shaped our history and orientation towards undeniable divine destiny and election prototyped by ancient Israel, is to give us a keener awareness of our enormous responsibility because to whom much is given much is required.

It is not coincidental that Torres was the first Jewish person to settle in the New World as a continuum of the ancient Jewish and Punic presence dating back to the trans-oceanic voyages during the Solo- monic times. In modern times, the first distinct Jewish settlement in America was in New Amsterdam in 1564, which later grew into pres- ent day N.Y. city. One cannot fail to see the divine design underlying the extraordinary fact that New York is the global financial center today. This can only be explained by the Abrahamic blessings. The story of America is a dramatic matrix that rises out of the fulfillment of ancient prophecies to Israel and played out in historical precedents.

America is a recipient of the Abrahamic covenant of blessings and its present manifestation through the multi-ethnic Protestants from the Old World, homogenized by a call to serve the Holy One of Israel as one nation under God, indivisible.

The Puritans, the first English Colonists, were steeped in ideas and cadences of the ancient Hebrew Bible. They modeled everything after ancient Jewish national ideas. Benjamin Franklin proposed that the seal for the United States show the Israelites crossing the red sea and Pharaoh's chariots in vain pursuit. Thomas Jefferson said, "Rebellion to tyrants is obedience to God, based upon the story of Moses." Samuel Fisher wrote in the Testimony in Trust 1679, "Let Israel be our mirror to view our faces in." John Winthrop wrote:

> *"We shall find that the God of Israel is among us,*
> *when ten of us shall be able to resist a thousand of our*
> *enemies, when He shall make us a praise and glory, that*
> *men of succeeding plantations shall say, The Lord make*
> *it like that of New England. For we must consider that*
> *we shall be a city upon a hill."*

These are weighty matters that heighten our vision, broaden our horizons, inspire us to greatness and beckon us to blaze a new trail, in the traditions of ancient Israel, as a chosen people. Ours is an extraordinary voyage through the sea of humanity, anchored in historical precedents.

Chapter Seven

EUROPEANS PRESENT IN AMERICA 3000 YEARS AGO

The European Celtic people were part of Solomon's global subjects. Tarshish was the farthest western Phoenician seaport in Andalusia, Southern Spain. The Greeks called it Turtessos. The Celtic Basques settled there. It became known as Cardiz. The Solomonic Phoenician merchants made it their trans-Atlantic embarkation port. About 2500 years later, Columbus set sail from the same area on his voyage to the New World like his ancient predecessors, who called the New World (the West) the land of the setting sun. When the Bible refers to the land of the West, it's referring to America. There are many prophetic references to the West regarding the Jews in the end of days. History repeats itself.

> *"What is has already been, and what will be has been*
> *before; and God will call the past to account."*
> *Ecclesiastes 3:15*

The European presence in the New World during the Solomonic era to exploit gold for the temple of God in Jerusalem was a prelude to the present day linkage between the USA and Israel.

Professor Barry Fell believes that the Algonquian Indians speak a language akin to Basque Celtics of the Punic Bronze era. Though the pronunciation has been blurred by the passage of time, it is clear that it is a derivative of the Celtic tongue. The Gaelic Celtic alphabet, the ogam inscriptions, has been found in North America dating back to the bronze era signifying the significant contribution of the Japhetic people to the Solomonic global expansionism to the New World. They influenced the Algonquin Indian language. The Phoenicians and Hebrews had their last staging outpost amongst the Basque Celtics in Cardiz Spain before sailing o the New World. Some of the Basque Celtic people moved to the New World to establish trade posts with the Punic Hebraic merchants.

A derivative of a Semitic – Punic – Celtic language was spoken in Cardiz (or ancient Tharshish) and was exported to the New World. The Punic Celtics from Cardiz settled in New England Idajo where they elected temples of stone. The gravestone inscription in Iberian Punic letters spells the names Arano or Eagle in Basque language.

This is the first time the eagle is associated with America in extra Biblical record in ancient times. The book of Isaiah refers to the land of the eagle 700 years before Christ.

> *"Woe to the land of eagles wings" Isaiah 18:1*

The eagle was the symbol of America (Arano) 3000 years ago during the Celtiberian, Phoenician, Semitic occupation in the Bronze era. America was known as the land of the setting sun, symbolized by the eagle in the ancient times. Solomonic trans-Atantic trade involved the Basque Celtic inhabitants of Tharshish or Cadiz in Southern Spain. Isaiah mentioned Tarshish in his prophecy regarding a land that the Jews will settle in the distant future. Tarshish was a destination of ancient ships from Cardiz during Solomonic exploration.

> *"I will set a sign among them, and I will send some of those who survive to the nations – to Tarshish They will glory among the nations." Isaiah 66:19*

Ezra Stile, who later became President of Yale, discovered in 1780 at Mount Hope, Rhode Island an incised figure of a high-sterned

Tartessian hull engraved on a rock and an inscription "Mariners of Tarshish this rock proclaim." Professor Barry Fell of Harvard and Rommel and Germano deciphered the inscription.

The Bible, for instance, refers to Tarshish as a real place in distant lands abroad.

> *"But Jonah rose up to flee unto Tarshish from the presence of the Lord, and went down to Joppa; and he found a ship going to Tarshish: so he paid the fare thereof, and went down into it, to go with them unto Tarshish from the presence of the Lord." Jonah 1:3*

The prophet Jeremiah refers to it as a distant land rich in metals known to ancient Hebrews.

> *"Hammered silver is brought from Tarshish and gold from Uphaz." Jeremiah 10:9*

Herodotus identifies Tarshish with Tartessus in Southern Spain. Conclusive evidence comes from Sardina Spain where monumental inscriptions erected by the Phoenicians in the Bronze era bear the name, Tarshish. W.F. Albright suggested that the word Tarshish comes from an Akkadian rasasu meaning to melt and the word tarsisu means melting-plant or refinery. Hence any place where mining and melting took place could be known as Tarshish, which would include ancient America.

THE AFRICANS IN THE AMERICAS 3000 YEARS AGO

During the Solomonic golden age of exploration, Hamitic or African people were part of the voyage to the New World to exploit gold for the Temple in Jerusalem together with the other Mediterranean people groups. Coptic Libyan and North African inscriptions have been discovered in North America, which date to the bronze era.

Historically the Africans were in America before the slave trade, according to Professor Barry Fell. In 1874, the Coptic Libyan Iowan text was found. Other Libyan Berber inscriptions have been found in New Hampshire, Pennsylvania, Quebec and Oklahoma. An inscription with an African elephant was found in Cuenca Ecuador. The knowledge of the elephant in the New World came from Africa. A Coptic Libyan inscription was found by Forrest Kirkland in Nubian under a hanging rock at Rio Grande cliffs in Texas that read "A crew of Shishong, the King took shelter in this place of concealment." Several monarchs with that name ruled Libya North Africa and Ethiopia between 1000- 800 BC.

In America, BC Harvard Prof. Fell tells of the African elephant pipe- bowl that was found at Davenport Mounds. Dr. Edward J. Pullman of the US Exploration Company found a Libyan – Coptic inscription on a mountain range adjacent to Mojave desert which reads: "All men, take care Great Desert."

Professor Fell believes that the Zuni Indian language is derivative of a North African language spoken in Southern Libya. The Shiwi and Zuni people are most likely to be descendents of ancient North African blacks. Ancient Libyan inscriptions have been found as far away as Polynesia in the Pacific. The Egyptian mined gold in Sumatra during the bronze era.

The Solomonic Mediterranean f leet employed Nubians, Libyans and Egyptians, Basque Celtics, in global exploitation of gold for the temple in Jerusalem in fulfillment of God's promise to Abraham that, "through you all the families of the earth will be blessed." This was the most sacred and holy task for mankind that extended blessings to the entire world as God promised Abraham.

Chapter Eight

AMERICA'S MANIFEST DESTINY

We need to look at the big picture to understand the historical impact of Solomon in the ancient world. As we observe the panoramic landscape, we are stunned to see His global footprint from such a small kingdom. They had a big God who gave them the world.

It is absolutely clear; the Solomonic merchants traversed the farthest corners of the earth and crisscrossed vast oceans. The question is, in what other parts of the world did they leave a permanent historic marker to authenticate this claim to world domination?

It is important that we begin by identifying who King Solomon is, how he became a global power in the ancient world about 3000 years ago, and how he explored the whole world, extending his influence. He was a son of David–a man after the heart of God – to whom God gave the divine right of Kings.

HIS MAJESTY KING MONOMOTAPA
Son of Solomon

"And when He had removed him (Saul) He raised up unto them David to be their king; to whom also He gave their testimony, and said, I have found David the son of Jesse, a man after mine own heart, which shall fulfill all my will..." Acts 13:22

"But King Solomon shall be blessed, and the throne of David shall be established before the Lord forever." Kings 2:45

King David, before he died, appointed and anointed Solomon as king. He prayed to God for wisdom and God granted him more than his request.

> *In that night did God appear unto Solomon, and said unto him, ask what I shall give thee. And Solomon said unto God, Thou hast showed great mercy unto David my father, and hast made me to reign in his stead. Now, O Lord God, let thy promise unto David my father be established: for thou hast made me king over a people like the dust of the earth in multitude. Give me now wisdom and knowledge, that I may go out and come in before this people: for who can judge this thy people, that is so great? And God said to Solomon, Because this was in thine heart, and thou hast not asked riches, wealth, or honor, nor the life of thine enemies, neither yet hast asked long life; but hast asked wisdom and knowledge for thyself, that thou mayest judge my people, over whom I have made thee king: Wisdom and knowledge is granted unto thee; and I will give thee riches, and wealth, and honor, such as none of the kings have had that have been before thee, neither shall there any after thee have the like." 2 Chronicles 1:7-12*

God made him the wisest man that ever lived. The whole world went to Jerusalem to hear his wisdom:

> *"And men of all nations, from all the kings of the earth who had heard of his wisdom, came to hear the wisdom of Solomon." 1 Kings 4:34*

Solomon had 1,000 women and 600 sons. He sent one of his sons with each of the rulers that came to see him. He appointed his sons to rule the nations. His family alone claimed the divine right of Kings. This explains the existence of the Jacobite Kings of Europe such as King James who authorized the translation of the King James Bible which was the single most important and ominous event – and event that changed the world and led to the founding of America by people who wanted to follow the Bible and came to the New World for religious liberty.

There is a false assumption that Solomon had a limited sphere of in- f luence in the Middle East. The divine right of Kings was not limited to Israel alone but was universal. He established the framework of today's globalization.

One of the most celebrated ancient descendants of Solomon is Monomotapa, a Jacobite King who built the edifices of Great Zimbabwe in the country between two rivers- the Limpopo and the Zambezi–known in ancient times as the land of Ophir. King Solomon appointed him over the royal gold resources needed to build the Temple. He built the stone city after the Jerusalem blueprint 1780 acres to house nearly 20,000 gold smith Jews to refine gold. The only mines discovered by the British when they colonized Rhodesia were the 1,000 ancient gold mines dating back to Solomonic times.

It should be noted that the ancient world knew of the gold in the land of the Jacobite King Monomotapa. It led to the Boer war to stop the Dutch from crossing the Limpopo river from South Africa to take possession of this land of gold. The British won and took incalculable amounts of gold which resulted in giving them the present prestigious position to fix the price of gold. Even though they have no gold mines in England, the British posses the Solomonic gold from Rhodesia.

The name of the Jews in Zimbabwe morphed from Shem to Shona. Interestingly, it is also a derivative of Sona, which means "land of gold" in the Indian language. They sold silk from China to Monomotapa. He became known as Chirimahazu (Anglicized) and Chilimanzi, which means, in Shona, "the man in the royal robe, the Jacobite King." I am a direct descendant of Chilimanzi the Son of Monomotapa, son of Solomon, son of David. I am an heir to the Davidic anointing. The blessings of God are irrevocable.

> *"For the gifts and calling of God are without*
> *repentance." Romans 11:29*

The primary thing that identifies Monomotapa as a Jacobite King is the crown, as no king except in the Middle East in the ancient times wore a crown. The tradition spread from there. Monomotapa brought the Levites to Great Zimbabwe to conduct the worship of Yahweh. This is the reason why, when missionaries came to Rhodesia, the Shona people did not worship idols. They knew that there is only One true God, whom they call Mwari the Creator. Recently the Lemba tribe in Zimbabwe has been tested and proven to be the descendant of Levi. This further authenticates the validity of this historical fact. A startling discovery was made of a replica of the ancient Ark of covenant in Zimbabwe (formerly Rhodesia) by Prof. Tudor Parfih after a worldwide search for several years.

Since our bias and prejudices color how we perceive things, only the Scriptures can dispel our illusions. As we all know, the ancient historical topography is literal with distortions and fragmentations. Only the scriptures can provide an immovable landmark, particularly in these ancient pathways. This whole matter constitutes a paradox embedded in history. The question that demands answers is, does the Bible have a reference to the Jews living beyond the rivers of Ethiopia, the Zambezi? It does indeed! The prophet Zephaniah addresses an offering that will be brought to God from these dispersed Jews at Gods appointed time.

> *"From beyond the rivers of Ethiopia my suppliants, even*
> *the daughter of my dispersed, shall bring mine offering."*
> *Zephaniah 3:10*

This is irrefutable evidence of the Monomatapa dynasty living beyond the rivers of Ethiopia in Zimbabwe.

There is undeniable evidence that points to a specific timetable in which these events took place during the Solomonic era of global exploration and gold exploration. The fact is that these ancient global travels and merchants left historical marks in America. The Los Lunas inscription and the Great Zimbabwe ruins are evidence that there is a correlation between the Bible and ancient history. As we observe the similarities, it becomes obvious that these historical facts present startling proof of the amazing achievements of Israel during the golden age. There are no coincidences in history as there is nothing new under the sun according to the scripture.

> *"That which hath been is now; and that which is to be hath already been; and God requireth that which is past." Ecclesiastes 3:15*

The focus of this book is America's past and future. I have given his- torical evidence that the Solomonic Kingdom had global influence in other parts of the world. It was not just America. The thing that makes America unique is the Los Lunas Decalogue inscription. It made America special.

The pre-eminence of America is grounded and rooted in the unal- terable and irrevocable blessings established from ancient times ac-cording to the scriptures. The blessings of God last for a thousand generations.

> *"Therefore know that the Lord your God, He is God, the faithful God who keeps covenant and mercy for a thou- sand generations with those who love Him and keep His commandments." Deuteronomy 7:9*

It is upon this presumption that I believe America is still blessed. The covenantal blessings of God are conditional and based upon obedience. I envisage America repenting and restored to her greatness. I have a great hope, based upon faith in God, that the future will be dominated by godly men and free from adversarial intelligence that opposes God's moral standard. I am praying for America to return to God and, purged of its sin, will stand together as one nation under God, blessed and highly favored.

Chapter Nine

ISAIAH PREDICTED AMERICA'S SUPPORT FOR ISRAEL

> *"The steps of the righteous are ordered by the Lord."*
> *Psalm 37:23*

Christopher Columbus's discovery of the New World was not by chance. The whole phenomenon rose out of a profound understanding of ancient predictions encoded in Hebrew sacred literature. Columbus's voyage can be summed up concisely as an act of obedience to inner impulses and leadings that were far stronger than the popular rationale of the leading intellectual community of his day.

The spirit of God came upon him as it did upon Moses when he saw the burning bush in the Holy pages of the scripture. He became af lame with a prophetic passion. He was convinced beyond any shadow of doubt that he had received divine illumination and that his voyage was a divine mission to fulfill the Holy Scriptures.

Christopher's writings provide a prophetic basis that explains why events happened the way they did. He gives vivid, perceptive, un- deniably authoritative analogies reminiscent of his sense of divine guidance during his voyage to the Indies. In his book of prophecies, "Libro de cas profecias," he wrote:

> *It was the Lord who put into my mind (I could feel His*
> *hand upon me) the fact that it would be possible to sail*

> *from here to the Indies. All who heard of my project re-*
> *jected it with laughter, ridiculing me.*
>
> *There is no question that the inspiration was from the*
> *Holy Spirit because He comforted me with rays of mar-*
> *velous illumination from the Holy Scriptures, a strong*
> *and clear testimony from the 39 books of the Old Tes-*
> *tament, from the four gospels and from the 23 epistles of*
> *the blessed apostles, encouraging me continually to press*
> *forward and without ceasing for a moment they now*
> *encourage me to make haste.*

God led Christopher Columbus to the new world because the appointed time had come for God to raise up a nation from many nations, homogenized by a divine call to be a light to the nations. This is
clearly expressed in Columbus writings, when he wrote:

> *"Our Lord Jesus desires to perform a very obvious mir-*
> *acle in the voyage to the Indies, to comfort me and the*
> *whole people of God."*

America's manifest destiny is to comfort the whole people of
God, both Jew and the persecuted saints in Europe. The founding
fathers shared this same sense of destiny. The idea they espoused was
exten- sively influenced by the paradigm of ancient Israel. They saw
them- selves as the new Israel, chosen and set apart by the divine sovereignty. They heavily relied on divine providence to prevail over their
enemies like Israel of old.

From Columbus's famous voyage to this present day, God has
be- stowed upon America amazing grace that transcends and pervades
the whole tapestry of American history. In 1789, George Washington,
in his inaugural address, expressed concern that the American people
need to remain faithful to God and not to rebel against Him.

> *"The propitious smiles of heaven can never be expected on a nation that disregards the eternal values of order and right which heaven itself has ordained."*

Several of the founding fathers expressed the same sense of being a special nation in the family of nations, called to serve God in the common house of mankind. Abraham Lincoln warned his fellow Americans not to forget God, who had brought them this far.

> *"But we have forgotten God. We have forgotten the gracious Hand which preserved us in peace and multiplied and enriched and strengthened us; and we have vain- ly imagined in the deceitfulness of our hearts, that all blessings were produced by some superior wisdom and virtue of ours."*

Benjamin Franklin, in 1787, begged for prayers during the Constitutional Convention in humble submission to God and in acknowledgement that this nation's future was in the hand of God and not in the hand of men:

> *"I therefore beg leave to move that henceforth prayers imploring the assistance of heaven and its blessing on our deliberations be held in the Assembly every morning."*

The founding fathers of this nation were aware of America's divine destiny. It is this manifest destiny that gave them a sense of awesome responsibility. The prophetic role of America is as a divine instrument of his saving grace, as a comfort to the people of God inspired them to attempt the impossible.

The early American national ethos constituted a phenomenon exten- sively influenced by a unique sense of providential destiny, separate and peculiar in nature to that of any other nation on earth. This uniqueness was epitomized by her missionary passion. I am sure that this is part of what Columbus meant when he said:

> *"There are great and wonderful things for the earth and
> the signs are that the Lord is hastening the end. The fact
> that the gospel must still be preached to so many lands,
> in such a short time this is what convinces me."*

Beyond any shadow of doubt, America has a Biblical mandate to evangelize the World. There is no argument against the historical fact that most of the world has been evangelized by American missionary enterprise in fulfillment of her manifest destiny.

Chapter Ten

THE NEW WORLD WAS DISCOVERED AT THE KAIROS (APPOINTED) HOUR

> *"These are the feasts of the Lord holy appointed*
> *convocation which you shall proclaim at their appointed*
> *times." Leviticus 23:4*

The feasts of the Lord are divine appointments (Kairo). Almost all prophetic events throughout history took place at these appointed feasts of the Lord. All prophetic events have a precedent. The feasts of the Lord commemorate divine interventions in the affairs of man. He is Lord of history. Mankind has an appointment with God. All disappointment is missing divine appointment with destiny.

The fact that America and the New World were discovered at the time of the feast of the Lord, God's appointed time for manifest destiny, removes all doubt of whether or not America is chosen. This foundational fact undergirds and establishes indisputably America's manifest destiny. This is a historical truth. All doubters must now doubt their doubts.

The discovery of The New World followed the prophetic blueprint, tested and proven in 6000 years of written human history. God was paving the way for the raising of a people—terrible and mighty from the beginning—mentioned in the sacred book of Isaiah. The fact that Isaiah prophesied the rise of a powerful nation whose national sym- bol would be an eagle ages before confirms God'smanifest destiny for America. The discovery of the New World during the prophetic appointed times of the feast of the Lord further authenticates the fact that this nation's future is in God's hands.

Columbus, who is believed to have been of Jewish lineage, boarded the ship at midnight on Av 9 (August 2), 1492. Spain issued its "Final Edict" in March 1492 declaring that all Jews must convert to Catholicism or be banished. Midnight on August 2 was the deadline for all of the Jewish people to leave Spain. This was the seventh Jewish major disaster on Av 9. Here again we see prophetic precedent. At dawn on August 3, Columbus set sail. Here is how he describes his experience of this voyage to the New World.

> *"I could feel Gods hand upon me, the fact it would be*
> *possible to sail from here to the Indies. For the execution*
> *of the journey to the Indies. I did not make use of*
> *intelligence mathematics or maps. For it is simply the*
> *fulfillment of what Isaiah prophecied."*

Columbus described his voyage to the New World as simply a fulfillment of Isaiah's prophecies. God led Columbus–he could feel His hand upon him. The time had come for God to raise up a nation, whose national symbol would be an eagle, for the comfort of His people being persecuted in the old world, both Jews and evangelical Christians. Columbus, like Moses of old, led the people of God to a land of freedom from religious bondage of Europe to the land of promise. He was a Marrano, or secret Jew. Five of his crew as well as his interpreter were known to be Jewish.

Columbus discovered the New World on October 12, Tishri 1 on Hoshana Rabbah, the seventh day of Succot, the seventh feast of the Lord. The number seven expresses completeness of Gods plan. Seven is used 700 times in scriptures to express divine perfection. The discovery of the New World represents the perfect will of God at the perfect time. Seven also represents rest. America is a place for the troubled and persecuted people to find rest and enjoy freedom of religion.

The seventh day of the seventh feast known as Hoshana Rabbah, according to Jewish tradition was known as the day God decreed His blessings on His people for the future. The discovery of the New World was a quantum leap for the people of God into a new dispensation of freedom from religious persecution: a paradigm shift in world history. It was a moment that defined all future history. The ecclesiastical imperialism was nullified and a new age of Protestantism was born. This was a vital fact in altering the status quo. It was such a mega-event that it changed the course of the church and world history. The discovery of the New World was a consummation of a struggle between the totalitarian collectivism of the dark ages and individualism. America liberated the individual from the shackles and tyranny of conformity to empty religiosity of the Old World.

This brings us to a critical awareness that America's manifest destiny is not to politisize, democratize or privatize the world economy, but to bring the light of Jesus Christ to a dying world. The better we understand this, the better prepared we will be to fulfill our divine mandate to the world to set the captives free. Embedded in Christopher Columbus's name is America's mission. Christopher means the bearer of Christ's light.

The discovery of the New World on Hoshana Rabbah 1492, a day foreordained by God as a day of receiving divine favor, is a remarkable evidence to substantiate America's manifest destiny as the chosen and appointed nation to fulfill God's plan of the ages. On this same day, Tishri 1, in 1000 BC, the glory filled Solomon temple, in 536 BC. Exiles from Babylon began to rebuild the temple in Jerusalem and, in 445 BC, Ezra read the book of the law to the people of God. There is a definitive correlation between the feast of the Lord and the prophetic purpose of God on the earth. America has a prophetic destiny encoded in Hoshana Rabbah.

It is believed that on Hoshana Rabbah, Moses received the Torah from God for all mankind. God came from heaven to speak to Israel on Mt. Sinai. It was historic moment! A Kairos hour! A moment in eternity never to be forgotten! The whole world was changed by God's advent on Mt. Sinai. The Ten Commandments are the basis of civilization. They are divine absolutes. The notion that America can hold together without Biblical absolutes has been proven wrong throughout the centuries. Israel tried to hold on to manifest destiny in vain, having rejected God's law.

America is in danger of being transformed from a democracy to a mob-ocracy by the emerging pluralistic and ethnocentric citizenry that reject Judeo-Christian absolutes and embrace pagan values and strange customs and habits. The glue that holds America together is its manifest destiny, the shared assumptions of liberty and justice for all and a common morality handed to mankind on Hoshana Rabbah on Mt. Sinai.

God did not send Christopher Columbus to discover the New World in order to create a melting pot of paganism. Christopher clearly expressed the objectives of his voyage in his own writings concerning his journey with God to the Indies:

> *"The fact that the gospel must still be preached to so many lands in such a short time, this is what convinces me."*

America is called to be a base of global evangelism and not a pluralistic and pagan utopia. Hoshana Rabbah defines America's mission to carry the light of the Torah to the nations in this dispensation of grace.

Chapter Eleven

PARALLELISM IN THE DIVINE PURPOSE

> *"And we know that in all things God works for the good*
> *of those who love him, who have been called according*
> *to his purpose." Romans 8:28*

Here is a paradox; all major changes in human history came through crisis. Every paradigm shift in the world is engineered by forces derived from the perils inherent in the breakdown of the traditional order of things. The 1389 Turkish victory over the Serb Bogomils at the battle of Kosovo planted the seed for what was yet to come. In 1452, the Islamic forces of Mehmet II closed the Bosporus straits to the Christian west to travel to India via the east trade route. The Moors put Christendom in a stranglehold and contained the Christian giant from expanding its influence to the east and stopped Europe's trade with India and China. This was a major crisis for the western economy. This is the crisis that led to the discovery of the New World: Islamic aggression.

For 1400 years, there has been a conflict between an Islamic agenda of global domination and western civilization. The Moors invaded the Spanish and Portuguese Iberian Peninsula in 711 AD. The east- west conflict reached its apex in France and was turned back at the battle of Poitier by Charles Martel in 732 AD. The west struggled against Islamic domination in Europe for 781 years. In 995 AD, Russia became officially a Christian Orthodox country in order to unite and enable itself to fight against the Islamic hordes riding across the steppes, raping and pillaging.

Finally in 1492, in the same year that Columbus discovered the New World, Islamic control was overturned in Spanish Granada. Ironically, what the devil meant for evil, God used for his glory. The Islamizing and demonizing forces of evil were God's instrument to open up the New World for His people. America, which was born as a result of the Islamic Middle East policy of containment in 1452, led the coalition forces–nearly 425 years after Columbus–who defeated the Islamic Ottoman Empire in 1917. Christendom triumphed over Islam because of the New World and America in particular. A nation was birthed as a result of hostile Islamic policy. As always, what the devil meant for evil, God turned to good.

The current rise of Islamic radical extremism poses the same grave threat again to Judeo-Christian civilization. The fact is that the world continues to depend on Middle East oil in the hands of these radical Islamic regimes. The present oil crisis will lead to the dis- covery of renewable, alternative energy sources for the world. Again, Islam will force the west to new frontiers and new discoveries for the benefit of mankind.

We have completed a circle. We are back where we began from in 1452 and Islam is on the move again against western interests in the east. It is astonishing that, 552 years later, we find ourselves facing the same conditions. History is about to repeat itself. A threat to western inter- ests in the east is again looming in the wings. We are confronted with constant shutdowns, slowdowns, and downturns in oil output which is putting unbearable pressure on the western economy., Combined with irrational Islamic extremist global terrorism, this constitutes the pre-conditions that threaten a large-scale conflict between the east and the west. Islamic aggression is about to experience a major defeat and humiliation. Darkness cannot defeat light.

These developments point overwhelmingly to one conclusion: that America's manifest destiny entails God's plan to stop the most pernicious forces of evil from destroying western civilization. The lessons in history are unmistakable, we must contend with these forces of evil before they force the whole world into global wreckage and terminal chaos. America must not compromise; she must remain on God's side, faithful to her manifest destiny as a global leader in the struggle between the forces of good and evil.

Chapter Twelve

DIVINE REVELATION OF THE NEW WORLD

> *"He sits enthroned above the circle of the earth,*
> *and its people are like grasshoppers. He stretches out the*
> *heavens like a canopy, and spreads them out life a tent*
> *to live in." Isaiah 40:22*

The question remains: how did Christopher Columbus know that the earth was round against the fallacious assumptions of the whole world. The answer to this question can only be found in the infallible and irrefutable, predominantly Hebraic biblical insight: ***"He sits enthroned above the circle of the earth."*** (Isaiah 40:22) This prophetic perception ultimately determined and precipitated the Solomonic voyages and Columbus' voyage. This passage gave him the confidence and determination to sail westward against popular opinion. He wrote; "I did not make use of intelligence, mathematics, or maps. It is simply a fulfillment of what Isaiah had prophesied."

Ancient Biblical literature, in most cases, is coded and remains a paradox until one receives special illumination such as Christopher Columbus had before he undertook the voyage to the Indies. The implication of his actions harmonized with Biblical revelation led to a quantum leap in history. Today, 500 years later, we have a much broader picture of the importance of his simple determination to follow the persistent advocacy of his scriptural exegesis of this passage. His bold action was both transcendent and spontaneous. It remains one of the most significant milestones in history. This prophetic revelation opened the passage to the New World.

Have you ever wondered why Christopher Columbus sailed southwest, rather than straight westward? Christopher Columbus direction was not coincidental. It was determinative and definitive. Therefore, disregarding the derivative and subordinate circumstantial evidence of modern scholarship, the only explanation is found again in the book of Isaiah.

> *"Woe to the land shadowing with eagles wings, which*
> *is beyond the rivers of Ethiopia (overseas): That sendeth*
> *ambassadors by the sea, even in vessels of bulrushes upon*
> *the waters, saying, Go, ye swift messengers to a nation*
> *scattered and peeled, to a people terrible from their*
> *beginning hitherto; a nation meted out and trodden*
> *down, whose land the rivers have spoiled!"*
> *Isaiah 18:-1-2*

The direction of his voyage implies that he had profound insights into this passage imparted to him by God alone. Christopher Columbus had prophetic perception regarding the purposes of God, most of which he wrote in his book of prophecies regarding his mission.

God gave him insights into Isaiah's prophetic paradox. He understood that, in order to discover this new land, he must go westward on the same latitude that runs across ancient Ethiopia. He understood the word mistranslated to mean "beyond" in the English Bible comes from the Latin word, geond. As an Italian, he knew it meant, "across, over, farther off, far away, to the farther side of." He realized the suitable oceanic passage to the New World had to be between the tropic of cancer and 20 degrees latitude that runs across Ethiopia (the name the Hebrews called Black Africa outside of Egypt.)

The new land God was going to raise for his end time purpose—whose national symbol would be an eagle—was located *across over from Africa (Ethiopia) farther off, far away, to the farther side of Africa.* Across, over to the other side of the ocean. Columbus knew, from this passage, the global positioning of the voyage to the New World. This is why he traveled southwest on his voyage to the New World to 20 degrees latitude and also to obtain fresh supplies from the last known outpost in the Atlantic. It is crucial to observe that this "eagle Nation" was not part of Africa because it sends ambassadors by sea, even in vessels of bulrushes upon the waters. The evidence of such definitive geographic positioning further confirms a marvelous and obvious prophetic identification of the United States of America as the land of divine manifested destiny. In the view of such Biblical evidence, it is not surprising that Christopher wrote in his book of prophecy that he found these details that enabled him to find the New World in the book of Isaiah. This is what he personally said regarding the matter:

> *"The prophets wrote in various ways Isaiah is the*
> *one most praised by Jerome, Augustine, and by other*
> *Theologians. They all say Isaiah was not only a prophet*
> *but an evangelist as well. Isaiah goes into great detail in*
> *describing the future events"*

The historical tapestry of providence is irrefutable, from the time of Columbus to this day. It is striking to see the mighty Hand of God orchestrating all these monumental events to bring about His plan and purpose in history though a people called out from the nations to form one nation under God, beginning with Columbus's voyage. In difficult times like we are living in, this should heighten our sense of destiny, especially today, as our nation is experiencing a massive deconstruction and an alarming darkness and uncertainty has began to cloud our sense of mission in the world.

Chapter Thirteen

THE DIVINE MANDATE TO SUPPORT ISRAEL

> *"In that time a present will be brought to the Lord of*
> *hosts from a people terrible from their beginning onward:*
> *A nation powerful and treading down… to the place of*
> *the name of the Lord of hosts to Mt. Zion." Isaiah 18:7*

This prophecy predicted that America will be the greatest supporter of Israel. Today, Israel is our only democratic ally in the region. America has a moral responsibility to stand in solidarity with Israel. There is a growing Christian consciousness to align ourselves with our Hebraic roots. America's support for Israel has brought untold blessings upon this nation because God is a covenant keeping God. He told Abraham, "I will bless those who bless you and whoever curses you I will curse." As a result of America's support for Israel, God has opened the windows of heaven and blessed this nation beyond measure. America's gross national product equals that of 90 countries of the world. She is the only country to put men on the moon. America is the most powerful nation on the earth because God promised to bless those that bless Israel. As long as America aligns herself with Israel she will remain the richest country in the world.

Historical facts point overwhelmingly to one conclusion: that God blesses those that bless Israel and curses those that curse Israel. History bears record that every kingdom that went against Israel perished: Egypt, Assyria, Babylon, Medo Persia, Greece, Rome and Germany.

Isaiah foretold that America, the "eagle nation," will support Israel and be a recipient of the blessings of Abraham in the last days. The rebirth of Israel after 2000 years was ordained of God to make it possible for the fulfillment of this prophecy that *a present might be brought to the Lord of Host, from a people terrible from their beginning onward, a nation powerful that treads down its enemies.*

God raised America to protect Israel from the pernicious hatred of the modern state of Israel by Islamic extremists. This hatred has nothing to do with land for peace but an incomprehensible, built-in demonization of the Jews in the Koran.

In retrospect, we see a dramatic rise of America to prominence ever since the birth of Israel and its unwavering support for the modern state of Israel. America has stood against universal anti-Semitism, which is the devil's master plan to destroy God's cosmic plan of the ages and His covenant with Abraham to give his seed the Promised Land as an everlasting inheritance.

God, in His wisdom, foretold 2700 years ago America's destiny as Israel's ally. Isaiah's prophecy gives America a divine mandate to protect and provide resources for Israel. Isaiah, projected by the spirit, saw the rebirth of the state of Israel and America's role in the end-game. Perhaps the most haunting specter over our nation is America abandoning Israel and embracing the Arab agenda for oil reasons. When a nation departs from its manifest destiny, it is judged.

This is a critical hour in the history of America. Isaiah prophesied that our manifested destiny is to bring a present to Zion or Israel. Yet our foreign policies towards Israel have resulted in perpetuating endless circles of violence. Land-for-peace policy has failed. The conflict in the region must be understood within an Islamic cultural context and value system and not within the universal framework of the struggle for freedom. It is critical that the American people understand the basic tenets of Islamic jihad. Particular attention must be paid to the attributes peculiar to the Islamic people—derived from hundreds of years of influence by the Koran–which demonize the Jews. Islam has no room for accommodating the Jews.

Islamic fundamentalism is a fierce and powerful force, seeking to systematically undermine our manifest destiny to support the modern state of Israel. America is on a collision course with Islamic extremism. No matter how you cut it, there is not much time left before the whole Middle East explodes. America is facing a test of the will and it is at the crossroads. It must decide whether to remain faithful to its manifest destiny and *continue to bring a present to the Lord of Host in Zion*, stand firm with Israel, and face the approaching climatic showdown with Islamic international terrorism, possible oil embargo and inevitable economic decline, coupled with financial and military burden of protecting Israel. We must trust the Holy One of Israel to put heaven's shield upon our nation as we continue to stand in solidarity with Israel and avoid yielding to and appeasing the forces of evil that are hell-bound on destroying the modern state of Israel. If we betray Israel, the judgment of God will come upon us and we will go the way of ancient kingdoms that betrayed Israel, who ended up in the rubbish heap of bygone civilizations.

The threat of an oil embargo is the Arabs' weapon of choice against the American people. The radical elements in the Arab world are doing everything to create an amalgamation of oil producing states to raise the prospect of an oil embargo as a new front in their struggle to force America to betray Israel's inalienable right to the Promised Land. They hope that an oil embargo will ignite a universal hatred of the Jewish people in the west–especially in America–for causing a national energy crisis.

America has no choice but to remain faithful to its manifest destiny predicted 2700 years ago in the sacred scriptures that, from a people terrible a nation powerful from the beginning will bring a present to the Lord of hosts in Zion. This is our call. This is our divine mandate. This is our manifest destiny. This is the purpose for our existence. This is the reason for our unparalleled prosperity. This is why we are a sole superpower. We must not sell our birthright. We must remain faithful to the end.

The alternative of failing to pursue our manifest destiny is too frightening. It is unthinkable! This is what God says about the alternative: "The nation that forgets God shall perish." We must heed this warning from God.

Chapter Fourteen

THE CONSEQUENCES OF GOING AGAINST THE HOLY COVENANT

Do unto others, as you will wish them to do unto you.

As God has commissioned us to protect Israel and to bring an offer- ing to them, our policy should be based upon the law of reciprocity, derived from the Biblical imperative to "do unto others, as you would have them do unto you." This divine prerogative demands measures consistent with Arab actions opposed to the Holy Covenant God made with Abraham and his seed to give them the Holy Land as an inheritance forever. The policy of land for peace violates the Holy Covenant. It challenges divine sovereignty. It puts this nation on a collision course with the Almighty. If the Bible is true, which I be- lieve it is, we are treading on dangerous territory. God cares for the Arab people. He gave the children of Ishmael 12 nations and most of the world's oil resources. God is just. The plan of God is perfect.

He loves all the children of Abraham. Anti-Arab is anti-godly. The Bible is the road map to peace and stability, in the Middle East and the world.

The present policy of our government, in essence, as it appears, is merely a circumscription of the Arabs's unattainable demands which ignores the sacred and infallible Holy Covenant as revealed in the sacred scriptures.

The present policy of compromise and accommodation of Islamic extremist demands has proven costly and ineffective. The predominance of United States power in the world must align itself with the Holy Covenant to ensure divine reciprocity consistent with the promises ascribed to those who honor God's Holy word.

The United States' manifest destiny as one nation under God, chosen to protect the territorial integrity of the Holy Land, requires us to reorient our foreign policy towards Israel with the covenant-keepers in Israel and not the covenant-breakers who advocate for the land for peace policy.

The question in real politics is whether the Biblical solution to the Middle East political crisis is relevant today, more than 4000 years after God made a covenant with Abraham. This is the critical ques- tion. The decisive factor. The only issue. The crux of the matter. The answer to this question will resolve the whole Middle East crisis. Human answers cannot suffice, only the sacred scriptures can give us irrevocable, immutable, inerrant and infallible divine answers. Here is God's answer to this most troubling question today.

> *"And I will give unto thee, and to thy seed after thee, the land wherein thou art a stranger, all the land of Canaan, **for an everlasting possession; and I will be their God.**" Genesis 17:8*

> *"Thus saith the Lord, which giveth the sun for a light by day, and the ordinances of the moon and of the stars for a light by night, which divideth the sea when the waves thereof roar; The Lord of hosts is his name: If those ordinances depart from before me, saith the Lord, **then the seed of Israel also shall cease from being a na- tion before me for ever.** Thus saith the Lord; If heaven above can be measured, and the foundations of the earth searched out beneath, I will also cast off all the seed of Israel for all that they have done, saith the Lord."* Jeremiah 31: 35-37

The time has come for the remnant of righteous Americans to rise up and declare boldly: God said it! That settles the question of land for peace once and for all, no more compromise! Forever means forever! According to Biblical prophecy, this is America's manifest destiny in the endgame.

Chapter Fifteen

THE COLLAPSE OF THE FORMER SOVIET UNION A WARNING

SIMILARITY OF VISION

America's origin and history parallel that of Israel. This similarity is rich and extensive. The pilgrims called America the new Israel. Unfortunately, today the American people are treating this likeness passively and superficially and more often, it has simply been left unexplored. The time has come for America to have a renewed vision of its manifest destiny. The historical perspective of the pilgrims was, in large measure, a ref lection of Israel's journey from Egypt to the Holy Land–they saw theirs as a similar call.

The central trait of their protestant culture was an orientation towards other-worldly values. Like the Hebrews of old, they saw themselves as delivered by God to go to the Promised Land, to worship their God in spirit and truth. This American ethos f lourished and bound together a diversity of ethnicity; glued together by spiritual ties, a common vision and a sense of manifest destiny that created a qualitative difference, distinctly "American"–a new phenomenon in the family of nations. America is a nation bound together, not by historical ties of ethnicity but, by its manifest destiny.

Since America's inception, she has always stressed her uniqueness as one nation under God. The American faith in God is deeply embedded in its history. Most Americans still believe that God has a plan for America, like ancient Israel. For the first time, we can prove historically America's similarity to ancient Israel in order to substantiate this belief. The prophet Hosea, projected into the distant future, predicted the rise of a people on the earth that would declare themselves "One Nation Under God."

> *"And I will sow her unto me in the earth; and I will*
> *have mercy upon her that had not obtained mercy; and*
> *I will say to them which were not my people, Thou art*
> *my peo- ple; and they shall say, Thou art my God."*
> *Hosea 2:23*

The American ethic groups gathered from the nations were not orig- inally his people or children of the lineal descendants of Abraham, but Gentiles. Yet God says He will adopt them as His people and they will declare themselves as one nation under God. And they will say to the God of Abraham, "Thou art my God." No other nation has ever declared itself one nation under the God of Abraham on their currency. Hosea was prophesying about America and the church of God in the Diaspora.

PARALLELISM BETWEEN THE EXODUS AND COLUMBUS'S VOYAGE TO THE NEW WORLD

SIMILARITY IN DATES, 1492 BC (MOSES) 1492 AD (COLUMBUS)

In order to understand America's manifested destiny and its similarity to that of ancient Israel, one must look back at the incredible, indisputable, remarkable and compelling providence in her history. No other people, besides Israel of old, have ever experienced such bountiful blessings. There is an inextricable connection between Moses and Columbus. In 1492 BC, God delivered His people out of the bondage of the old world Egypt and led them to a new land to worship their

God in freedom and exactly in 1492 AD Columbus was raised by God to open the new world to the persecuted church, held in spiritual bondage in the old world and persecuted. Moses and the Israelites were of a type and were a shadow of America according to scripture:

> *"which are a shadow of things to come." Colossians 2:17*

God makes known his future plans in ancient types and shadows. This definitive timing confirms the parallel re-enactment of Moses's ancient story, chronicled in Columbus's monumental voyage, which repeats a vivid tapestry that inextricably bears the hallmark of divine sovereignty prototyped in the Exodus. It is a splendid masterpiece of astonishing prophetic fulfillment conceived in the heart of God. The origin of America resonates with a magnificent hope of a land of promise, whose manifest destiny was foreshadowed in the Exodus. The precision in the timing is overwhelming. Only God could do that to confirm His master plan for America from 1492 BC to 1492 AD.

PARALLELISM IN DELIVERANCE FROM AN OVERWHELMING ENEMY

As Moses and the children of Israel experienced major crisis, so did Columbus. The similarity bears the handiwork of God. The two men were called and anointed by the same spirit to open new possibilities for their people. The book of Exodus records an epic story of Israel stranded at the Red Sea and surrounded with the Egyptians in a perilous situation.

> *"So the Egyptians pursued them, all the horses and chariots of Pharaoh, his horsemen and his army, and overtook them camping by the sea beside Pi Ha-hi-roth, before Baal Zephon. And when Pharaoh drew near, the children of Israel lifted their eyes, and behold, the Egyptians marched after them. So they were very afraid, and the children of Israel cried out to the Lord. Then they*

> said to Moses, "Because there were no graves in Egypt,
> have you taken us away to die in the wilderness? Why
> have you so dealt with us, to bring us up out of Egypt?
> "Is this not the word that we told you in Egypt, saying,
> "Let us alone that we may serve the Egyptians"? For
> it would have been better for us to serve the Egyptians
> than that we should die in the wilderness." And Moses
> said to the people, "Do not be afraid. Stand still, and see
> the salvation of the Lord, which He will accomplish for
> you today. For the Egyptians whom you see today, you
> shall see again no more forever. The Lord will fight for
> you, and you shall hold your peace, And the Lord said
> to Moses, Why do you cry to Me? Tell the children of
> Israel to go forward. But lift up you rod, and stretch out
> your hand over the sea and divide it. And the chil- dren
> of Israel shall go on dry ground through the midst of the
> sea." Exodus 14:9-16

Christopher Columbus had an amazingly similar experience. On July 7, 1503, while shipwrecked and in pain, Christopher Columbus wrote about his afflictions in his Lettera Rarissima to the Sovereigns from Jamaica, not knowing whether anyone would read his letter:

> In January the mouth of the river became obstructed.
> In April, the vessels were all worm-eaten, and I could
> not keep them above water. At this time the river cut
> a chan- nel, by which I brought out three empty ships
> with con- siderable difficulty. The boats went back
> into the river for salt and water. The sea rose high and
> furious and would not let them out again.
>
> The Indians were many and united and attacked them
> and in the end killed them. My brother and all the rest
> of the people were living on board a vessel which lay in-

side. I was outside very much alone, on this rude coast, with a high fever and very fatigued. There was no hope of escape. In the state, I climbed painfully to the highest part of the ship and cried out for help with a fear- ful voice, weeping, to Your Highnesses" war captains, in every direction; but non replied. At length, groaning with exhaustion, I fell asleep, and heard a compassionate voice saying,

"O fool, and slow to believe and serve thy God, the God of every man! What more did He do for Moses and for David his servant than for thee? From thy birth He hath ever held thee in special charge. When He saw thee at man's estate, marvelously did He cause thy name to resound over the earth.

"The Indies, so rich a portion of the world, He gave thee for thine own, and thou has divided them as it has pleased thee. Of those barriers of the Ocean Sea, which were closed with such mighty chains, He hath given thee the keys. Thou was obeyed in so many lands, and thou hast won noble fame from Christendom. **What more did He do for the people of Israel, when he carried them out of Egypt**; or for David, whom from a shepherd He raised to be king over Judea?

"Turn thou to Him and acknowledge thy faults; His mer- cy is infinite; thine old age shall not hinder thee from performing mighty deeds, for many and vast heritages He holdeth. Abraham was past 100 when he begat Isaac, and Sarah was no young girl. Thou criest out for succor with a doubting heart.

"Reflect, who has afflicted thee so grievously and so often, God or the world? The privileges and promises which

> *God bestows, he doth not revoke; nor doth He say, after*
> *having received service, that this was not His intention,*
> *and that it is to be understood differently. Nor doth He*
> *mete out suffering to make a show of His might.*
>
> *"Whatever He promises He fulfills with interest; that is*
> *His way. Thus I have told thee what thy Creator hath*
> *done for thee and what He doth for all men. He hath*
> *now revealed a portion of the rewards for so many toils*
> *and dangers thou hast borne in the service of others."*

The Indians, like the Egyptians, wanted to eliminate the vision if it were not of Divine intervention. We are immortal until our work is over when we are in the service of the Holy One of Israel.

God made a way of escape as He did for Moses. He escaped the army of the Indian hordes seeking to kill him. Amazing similarity! Moses was sent to the natural seed of Abraham Israel, while Columbus was sent to rescue both the spiritual and natural seed of Abraham.

> *"However, the spiritual is not first, but the natural,*
> *and afterward the spiritual." 1 Corinthians 15:46*

First natural Israel, then spiritual Israel. The first dispensation of the law was territorially anchored in the Promised Land. Israel is the natural seed of Abraham and Christians are the spiritual seed of Abraham.

> *"And if you are Christ's, then you are Abraham's seed,*
> *and heirs according to the promise." Galatians 3:29*

Two people, two destinies—both chosen for a purpose to be fulfilled in history. In these final days of the dispensation of grace, the church of Jesus Christ—the spiritual Israel—is territorially based in America in its mission to win the lost world. This dichotomy defines American spirituality and its fervor for world missions.

The presumptions of America's forebearers, the founding fathers, were pre-eminently envisaged from its Biblical understanding of the divine order in history of first the natural, then the spiritual. The American idealism was a perception derived from its passion to realign its history and values with that of ancient Israel, as a modern counterpart. America is more than a people, it is an idea. A Biblical idea! It is this idea that homogenized the diverse people to pursue a call to be the light to the nations like Israel of old.

America and the Jewish people have a common calling, in the common house of mankind, to bear the light of God. It is a grave responsibility to be taken seriously.

AMERICAN INDEPENDENCE

In Biblical chronology, Abraham, the Patriarch from the Old World In Biblical Chronology, the year of Independence, 1776, was a year of Jubilee. According to God's word, it is the appointed time to proclaim liberty and to take back property that has been lost. The oppressed are set free. It's a time to celebrate freedom.

> *"And you shall consecrate the f if tieth year, and proclaim liberty throughout all the land to all its inhabitants. It shall be a Jubilee for you; and each of you shall return to his possession, and each of you shall return to his family. That f if tieth year shall be a Jubilee to you; in it you shall neither sow nor reap what grows of its own accord, nor gather the grapes of your untended vine." Leviticus 25:10-11*

The trumpet would be sounded to announce the year of Jubilee throughout the land. The American Liberty Bell is an iconic symbol of American independence. The history of America is intertwined with that of ancient Israel in an amazing way. The Liberty Bell is inscribed with a quotation from the King James version of the Biblical passage on Jubilee.

> *"And you shall consecrate the f if tieth year, and proclaim liberty throughout all the land to all its inhabitants. It shall be a Jubilee for you; and each of you shall return to his possession, and each of you shall return to his family." Leviticus 25:10*

It is not coincidental that the American independence was in the year of Jubilee as it was a divine act of God. The people that were oppressed by the British were set free. Jesus began his ministry in the year of Jubilee, to set mankind free. This is a Biblical paradigm.

It is believed that Joseph died in the year 1776 BC. It marked the end of an era. America severed its relationship with England and became independent. The young nation forged its own identity, ended British domination and took back its inalienable right to be free to pursue its own Manifest Destiny.

The Declaration of Independence was a major prophetic fulfillment. It was a monumental event of Biblical proportion. The tragedy is the fact that most American people are painfully ignorant of the ancient prediction regarding this historical event given thousands of years before. It is the only solid foundation to build the future upon. Here is America in Daniel's prophecy:

> *"The f irst was like a lion, and had eagle's wings. I watched till its wings were plucked off; and it was lifted up from the earth and made to stand on two feet like a man, and a man's heart was given to it."*
> *Daniel 7:4*

The lion represents Britain whose national symbol is the lion. The eagle was attached to it just as, historically, the colonies were connected to Great Britain, the lion nation. Daniel, projected into the distant future, saw the eagle on the back of the lion nation separated. On July 4, 1776, the eagle broke its relationship with the lion nation in a literal fulfillment of Daniel's prophecy. America's national symbol is an eagle. This prophecy forms the basis of American distinction. The Declaration of Independence was not just a declaration of liberation from the shackles of British imperialism but a divine appointment for America to embark on its national destiny.–a pathway conceived in the heart of God. Subsequently, providential history bears witness that God had separated the eagle.

As the prophet Daniel looked, the eagle morphed into a human figure with a human heart. What he was watching is an easily distinguish- able symbol in American culture: the Uncle Sam effigy. The human heart also represents Uncle Sam's compassion celebrated worldwide. Taken together, the American national symbol (the eagle) and Uncle Sam make it abundantly clear that Daniel was speaking about the United States of America. The breakaway of the eagle nation from the lion nation was a momentous event that would have immense implications in history.

Daniel saw the future from a divine vantage point revealed by the Author and Finisher of history. As we look back to the events during the War of Independence, we see God's intervention which made it possible to win the war. So, against this backdrop, we realize that the blessings, which we take for granted, are not achieved but received from God.

We are contending with growing public paranoia from those who reject the providential history of this country, who often refer to people who believe in it as unenlightened, fringe stereotypes and crackpots. They fail to realize that ancient Israel was destroyed when they turned their back on God. History repeats itself for those who fail to learn from the past.

There exists a stunning similarity between ancient Israel and America indicative of a divine calling on both peoples. Israel lost everything because she forgot God, who had set her free from Egypt. He made Israel a super power in the ancient world, prosperous, prestigious and indivisible yet when it forgot its divine calling and destiny God judged it. We face the same danger.

I cannot emphasize enough: any observer of history cannot fail to see that the tapestry of American history correlates precisely and resembles that of ancient Israel in divine predestination that demands total obedience to God. America is spiritually exhausted and sliding into the moral abyss similar to what happened to Israel. Only revival can save America. The claim to choiceness is meaningless when you abandon the God that chose you. We are facing monumental challenges that require divine intervention yet we are too prideful to humble ourselves and pray. We are living in a solemn period in history. World opinion is shaping our moral compass rather then the word of God.

Today we are facing, like Israel of old, spiritual and moral erosion that led Israel to judgment. There are signs everywhere that we are about to be judged like Israel. The current socio-political crisis we are facing is of epic proportions if we do not turn back to God.

America must learn from ancient Israel the folly of doing things her own way. This is the pathway to destruction.

PARALLELISM IN APOSTASY

The America of today has lost its manifest destiny and is submerged in the tidal wave of meaningless multiculturalism like Israel of old. The notion that America is one nation under God has been lost and replaced by universalism and pluralism. Contemporary America believes that her greatness is because of her democratic values. The downfall of Israel came when they sought universal accommodation and pluralism. America is being demonized and apostatized by the forces of multinationalism. Pluralism is always a snare to the chosen people of God. This is what led Israel to its downfall: cultural mixture.

The secular rationale that America will hold together without God has been tried before by Israel and it failed. It will fail again. The American left espouses secularism as apostatized ancient Israel did. They seek to distort the doctrine of church and state separation to demand that the church be alienated from the politics of the public square and openly deny God a place in the affairs of the nation. Israel denied God's rightful place in the public affairs of the nation after God blessed them abundantly and God in turn abandoned them.

Until the present day, America's uniqueness was not merely optimized by prosperity and military prowess, but mainly by the ecclesiology's participation in the public square. The influx of pagan cultures into the mainstream is precipitously downgrading and eroding this nation's spirituality and shifting the ethos of the people from their manifest destiny to meaningless existence and hedonism.

Chapter Sixteen

ISRAEL AND AMERICA'S COMMON DESTINY TO BE A LIGHT TO THE NATIONS

God's call is always redemptive for all nations. God elected Israel to perform a special service to mankind. He clearly explains His sovereign purpose for His election to them.

> *"For you are a holy people to the Lord your God; the Lord your God has chosen you to be a people for Himself, a special treasure above all the peoples on the face of the earth. The Lord did not set His love on you nor choose you because you were more in number than any other people, for you were the least of all peoples; but because the Lord loves you, and because He would keep the oath which He swore to your fathers, the Lord has brought you out with a mighty hand, and redeemed you from the house of bondage, from the hand of Pharaoh king of Egypt. Therefore know that the Lord your God, He is God, the faithful God who keeps covenant and mercy for a thousand generations with those who love Him and keep His commandments;" Deuteronomy 7:6 -9*

Israel was called to be a light to the nations or heathens. When Israel failed its mission, she was judged. It is not a small thing to be called by God. Like Moses of old, Christopher Columbus wrote what God told him regarding America's divine mission. According to Columbus's personal log, God's purpose in leading him to the New World was similar to ancient Israel:

> *"... to bring the gospel of Jesus Christ to the heathens"*

America has a divine mission just like Israel of old to be pathfinders, to liberate the human soul from the tyranny of collective paganism and conformity to empty ritualism, and formalism of empty religiosity. Jesus says to His church in the world:

> *"You are the light of the world. A city on a hill cannot be hidden." Matthew 5:14*

> *"and has made us to be a kingdom and priests to serve his God and Father" Revelation 1:6*

God made Israel a light to the nations to proclaim the law of God and to turn the nations from paganism to the true God. They failed their mission. During this dispensation of grace He sent the church, centralized in America in the New World, to carry out His message of redemption to the nations. This is what Columbus meant when he wrote about America's mission:

> *"I said that some of the prophecies remain yet to be fulfilled. These are great and wonderful things from the earth, and the signs are that the Lord is hastening the end. The fact that the gospel must still be preached to so many lands in such a short time, this is what convinces me."*

This nation's divine mission to the world defines the whole tapestry of the American providential history. If America is to continue to lead the world, she must know her mission bestowed upon her by divine sovereignty. Early America was extensively influenced by its gospel mission to the world. Judeo-Christian ethics, universal brotherhood and the Fatherhood of God, as taught in the Holy Scriptures, shaped the American psyche. The present uncertainty and ambiguity in American society is a clear indication that America has lost the path. America is lost in a lost world.

Chapter Seventeen

PARALLELISM IN ECONOMIC PROSPERITY BETWEEN ANCIENT ISRAEL AND MODERN AMERICA

God promises to prosper His people on the condition that they obey Him. This is a universal prerequisite for divine providence of abundance:

> *"But just as all the good things that the Lord your God promised concerning you have been fulfilled for you, so the Lord will bring upon you all the evil things, until he has destroyed you from off this good land that the Lord your God has given you, 16 if you transgress the covenant of the Lord your God, which he commanded you, and go and serve other gods and bow down to them. Then the anger of the Lord will be kindled against you, and you shall perish quickly from off the good land that he has given to you." Joshua 23:15-16*

God blesses America like Israel of old. Today, America is the richest country in the world and also the most powerful. The general–but wrong–conclusion is that wealth and power has made this nation great. America's greatness is in her faith in providentiality.

Israel rose above all the nations of the world and became the richest and a sole superpower on earth in their golden age, just like America today, because of God's favor. There is nothing new under the sun. The greatness of the Solomonic era foreshadows that of America today.

> *"So King Solomon surpassed all the kings of the earth in riches and wisdom. And all the kings of the earth sought the presence of Solomon to hear his wisdom, which God has put in his heart. Each man brought his present: articles of silver and gold, garments, armor, spices, horses, and mules, at a set rate year by year. Solomon had four thousand stalls for horses and chariots and twelve thousand horsemen whom he stationed in the chariot cities and with the king at Jerusalem. So he reigned over all the kings from the River to the land of the Philistines, as far as the border of Egypt. **The king made silver as common in Jerusalem as stones,** and he made cedar trees as abundant as the sycamores, which are in the lowland. And they brought horses to Solomon from Egypt and from all lands." Chronicles 9:22-28*

Like Israel, we are living in America's golden age. We have more chariots and horsepower than any other nation. Unprecedented wealth in the hands of merchant kings. America has much to learn from ancient Israel if we are to avoid following in their footsteps to oblivion. Pride goes before a fall. Without a vigorous effort to renew our commitment to God, America will implode from corporate corruption, greed and political interest groups with no moral restraint taking over the reigns of our democratic government. Human depravity always turns divine providence into consumerism and the worship of materialism. Man always cherishes the gifts rather than the Giver. Israel was overwhelmed and destroyed by its abundance and its position of power in the community of nations; pride led them to forget their God.

Chapter Eighteen

PARALLELISM IN SPRITUAL BANKRUPTCY BETWEEN ISRAEL AND AMERICA

The Old Testament is first and foremost a presentation of God's dealings with Israel as His chosen people. It centers upon God's actions in the affairs of men as He responds to Israel's spiritual condition. In essence, history is a revelation of the consequence of man's spiritual state.

When Israel apostatized, He judged them and when they obeyed, He blessed them. Israel's sin came between God and themselves. God's controversy with His people is always over sin which breaks down the covenantal relationship with Him and robs the people of God of covenantal blessings. Israel's religious leaders were always vanguards of the rebellion against God. They kept the form of religiosity without reality. God did not accept displays of religion without corresponding moral standards. The Pharisees and Sadducees would go to the extreme of maintaining the outward status quo while compromising the Holy standard, which they preached to the people. Isaiah's description of an apostatized Israel ref lects America's moral condition today when he says:

> *"But you iniquities have separated you from your God;*
> *And your sins have hidden His face from you, So that*
> *He will not hear. For your hands are defiled with blood,*
> *and your f ingers with iniquity; Your lips have spoken*

> *lies, Your tongue has muttered perversity. No one calls*
> *for justice, No does any plead for truth. They trust in*
> *empty words and speak lies; They conceive evil and*
> *bring forth iniquity." Isaiah 59:2- 4*

America is experiencing the same spiritual deception masquerading as the truth, having a form of godliness devoid of the presence of God. Today, the American spiritual spectrum is dominated by falsehoods, immorality, contradictions, seduction, bizarre doctrines of demons, delusions, salvation without repentance, happiness without holiness and sanctification without sacrifice. Money-lovers more than lovers of God, blind leaders leading the blind, pretenders, people-pleasers rather than God-pleasers, prophets for profit, wolves in sheep's clothing, preaching sermonettes to Christianettes. The Apostle Paul accurately foretold the conditions of the church in our nations in this terminal generation when he said:

> *"But know this, that in the last days perilous times*
> *will come: For men will be lovers of themselves, lovers*
> *of money, boasters, proud, blasphemers, disobedient to*
> *parents, unthankful, unholy, unloving, unforgiving,*
> *slanderers, without self-control, brutal, despises of good,*
> *traitors, headstrong, haughty, lover of pleasure rather*
> *than lovers of God. Having a form of godliness but*
> *denying its power. And from such people turn away!*
> *For of this sort are those who creep into households and*
> *make captives of gullible women loaded down with sins,*
> *led away by various lusts, always learning and never*
> *able to come to the knowledge of the truth."*
> *2 Timothy 3:1-7*

PARALLELISM IN DIVINE JUDGMENT BETWEEN ISRAEL AND AMERICA

> *"Therefore I also will act in fury. My eye will not spare*
> *nor will I have pity: and though they cry in My ears*
> *with a loud voice, I will not hear them." Ezekiel 8:18*

God's judgment is sure. Sin will be punished. History bears witness to the fact that God is just and faithful and that He keeps His word throughout the ages. He judged Israel for her rebellion and He will judge America if we do not repent from our sins. It is not too late to repent and turn back to God.

> *"If my people who are called by my name will humble*
> *themselves and pray and seek My face and turn from*
> *their wicked ways, then I will hear from heaven, and*
> *will forgive their sin and heal their land."*
> *2 Chronicles 7:14*

I believe that 911 was a wake up call to the carnal and compromised church in our nation. The church needs to move beyond social and political activism as a stop-measure and a panacea to our miserable spiritual predicament.

America is in a decline at its greatest moment in history. It is my conviction that the present conservatism backlash is a result of social reformation without transformation. The church is asleep at the switchboard. There is no voice in the wilderness calling for repentance from our sins. It is no coincidence that, in spite of the rise of conservatism in America, there is an increase in divorce, abortions, crime in urban America, corporate corruption, prison population explosion and drug addiction.

The main emphasis of mainline and mainstream American evangelicalism is an advocacy for political conservatism, external holiness without inner transformation–a tried and failed form of the "City of God" paradigm. This model of legalism without the transforming grace of God has been tried and failed miserably by ancient Israel. The problem with America today is a preoccupation with form rather than reality. America's manifest destiny requires the embodiment of Christ in every structure of society. The call of this nation is for the sole purpose of serving God's people on earth by empowering the poor, doing justice and proclaiming the gospel of the kingdom.

The tragedy in America today is a powerless, money-hungry, self-centered and self-serving church. A church that aligns itself with the ruling elite at the exclusion of the marginalized outcasts. Jesus indicted the religious leadership of His day for identifying themselves with the rich and the famous. The true people of God must seek to affect the social structures with the power of God. If America is to avoid the judgment of God that fell upon Israel, she must depart from the dogma of evangelicalism with its prescribed ritualism of empty formalism and its love affair with money. The church in America is on life support on its deathbed. In the early church history, the Christians were known as "the people of the way." The church is supposed to be the custodian of America's manifest destiny and a people of the way. Unfortunately, the church has lost the way.

The Pax Americana masks the ominous fact that the global village is becoming more and more dangerous to live in because the church is not doing its work of transforming nations. The American Army is not the answer to world's problems, but Jesus of Nazareth. We are called to be a light to the nations. This does not mean that American military power has no role to play in the erosive and unraveling world community because, to him much is given much is required. The problem is that the church is not fulfilling its critical responsibility to bring the transforming power of the gospel to a dying world because only changed lives will change our world.

America is trying to sell to the world a by-product of Biblical Christianity in vain, because democracy without Judeo-Christian values is an impossible dream. This has attributed to the scapegoating and refusal by world leaders to take responsibility for their actions and blaming America for all their failed policies. America is not the source of world problems. America's problem is trying to solve world problems by democratizing the pagan world. Democracy without Judeo-Christian values will not work. Only changed people can change society and operate a just society. Christendom is the basis of democracy.

America needs to return to its foundations. The bogus values of mate- rialism will not be able to sustain America in the face of the impend- ing forces of evil seeking to destroy this nation. Israel was eradicated as a nation when it went astray. There are profound effects on the future of the world depending on the direction America takes today.

The problem with America today is a pre-occupation with the Ameri- can dream and material well-being rather than spirituality. The social dilemma we are facing is a backlash of feeding our children Godless capitalism, pornography and a steady diet of television violence.

America must learn from Israel's history. Divine judgment is inevitable. God is in control of world history. We are facing signs that are pointing to scenarios of unpredictable international intrigue that could ignite global conflict of Biblical proportions. America's pursuit of global peace will coincidentally crash and bankrupt her. The burdens of the world are too big for one nation to bear. Only Jesus can save the world and carry its burdens It is already obvious, yet not surprising, that America is already looking for ways to escape the burden of obligation to play savior to the world. It is too expensive and too dangerous. America will soon want out. All ancient kingdoms collapsed under the weight of policing the world without God. Egypt, Assyria, Babylon, Medo Persia, Greece, Rome, and—in modern times—the British Empire. We are fast approaching this point of exhaustion. It is at this breaking point that western civilization will collapse and give way to global upheaval of apocalyptic proportions

THE COLLAPSE OF THE FORMER SOVIET UNION A WARNING TO THE UNITED STATES OF AMERICA

> *"The wicked shall be turned into hell, and all the nations that forget God." Psalm 9:17*

The collapse of communism was not a triumph of free enterprise, democracy and capitalism but the fulfillment of God's warning to any civilization that turns away from God.

We see in America remarkable similarities between communist Russia before its fall from the burden of atheism, humanistic materialism, secularism and liberalism. The removal of Biblical Christianity in favor of godless ideology in Russia in order to preserve political supremacy and total control of man–spirit, soul and body–is now a matter of shame. Communism tried in vain to play God and to replace Him with intellectualism and materialism.

The United States is struggling with the same spiritual decline that Russia experienced before the communist revolution. If America continues on this perilous pathway, it will end up in an inevitable collapse. America should realize that the decline of Russian predominance in the world was not because of military, economic, financial and social reasons, but was precipitated by its godless, delusional ideology. It is not absurd to believe that if America continues on the path of godless pluralism, conservatism and its empty religiosity, she could implode and collapse and cease from being a sole superpower in the world in our generation.

When we look back in History, we see that Israel's internal or external problems did not make or break her, but turning away from God. In our generation, we have watched history repeat itself in the stunning changes that occurred in the former Soviet Union. Godless capitalism is heading toward the historic, climatic destiny of every godless political system in our world that rejected God. The Holy Scripture warns us:

> *"Do not be deceived, God is not mocked; for whatever a man sows, that he will also reap." Galatians 6:7*

It is astonishing, but perhaps not surprising when you realize that the former Soviet Union has a disproportionate advantage over America. It has vast natural resources vital for both military and industrial supremacy, yet it lacked one vital thing that makes it all work. The missing dimension was the lack of spirituality. This is the critical factor in the life of every nation.

America, as a nation, is struggling through a similar spiritual crisis. This could be a decade of decay if we do not turn to God. We are already facing signs of things to come, such as unprecedented international terrorism, debt implosion, stock market bust, real-estate price plunge, Social Welfare insolence and financial and corporate instability. These are signs of perilous times ahead of this nation without divine intervention. It is time for the people of God to cease from standing on the sidelines, excusing themselves and accusing everyone for America's dilemma. We have watched helplessly as prayer was being removed from our Public Schools, the Ten Commandments from our public square and condoms being freely given to our children in public schools. The church is retreating from the battle ground for the future of our nation.

Those who advocate for a privatistic and quetistic religion and es- pouse the doctrine of church and state separation want to see the church leave the public square to demonizing forces of evil. This is not Biblical Christianity. Jesus is Lord of the public square. Jesus took the message out of the temple to the common man on the street and to the public square. The enemies of America's manifest destiny are dedicated to their agenda of secularizing and demonizing the fu- ture generations. They envision a godless republic, fashioned after the failed model of the former Soviet Union.

Communism marginalized the church and rendered it increasingly difficult to serve God openly. This pattern should only serve as a les- son to America and not be followed. From the beginning of the rise of communism, it had a paradigmatic, irrational and delusional political philosophy, predictably destined to create a defunct utopia of lost men unaware of their lostness. All of the conditions underlying the collapse of the former Soviet Union point to one single factor, that refusal of freedom of conscience and religion by a monopolized state power is a vain attempt to conquer the human quest for communion with God. There is a vacuum in every human heart that only God can fill. Tragically, America is following the footsteps of the former Soviet Union.

We are seeing, throughout the former Soviet Union, nations turning to God, having realized that nations do not exist because of economic and military power but by the grace of God. These spiritually marginalized and impoverished populations are calling on American missionaries to bring the good news of Jesus Christ to them today.

The task today is to restore America to its historical roots. America's manifest destiny is to model a nation envisioned by the founding fathers as expressed in the constitutions of the early colonies. It is time to look back and review some of these early documents if we are to find our way back home with God where we belong. Every constitution of the early colonies was God-centered. This was their ethos; this was their passion. This was their pursuit.

> *We the people of the State of Rhode Island and*
> *Providence Plantations, grateful to Almighty God for*
> *the civil and religious liberty which He hath so long*

> permitted us to enjoy, and looking to Him for a blessing
> upon our endeavors to secure and to transmit the same,
> unimpaired, to succeeding generations, do ordain and
> this Constitution of government.

The Constitution of the commonwealth of Massachusetts, preamble and Article II:

> We, therefore, the people of Massachusetts, acknowledging,
> with grateful hearts, the goodness of the great Legislator
> of the universe, in affording us, in the course of His
> providence, an opportunity, deliberately and peaceably,
> without fraud, violence or surprise, of entering into an
> original, explicit, and solemn compact with each other;
> and of forming a new constitution of civil government,
> for ourselves and posterity; and devoutly imploring
> His direction in so interesting a design, do agree upon,
> ordain and establish the following Declaration of Rights,
> and Frame of Government, as the Constitution of the
> Commonwealth of Massachusetts.
>
> Article II. It is the right as well as the duty of all men
> in society, publicly, and at stated seasons to worship
> the Supreme Being, the great Creator and Preserver of
> the universe. And no subject shall be hurt, molested, or
> restrained, in his person, liberty, or estate, for worshipping
> God in the manner and season most agreeable to
> the dictates of his own conscience; or for his religious
> profession or sentiments; provided he doth not disturb the
> public peace, or obstruct others in their religious worship.
> (See Amendments, Arts. XLVI and XLVIII)

Constitution of Maryland, Declaration of Rights:

We, the People of the State of Maryland, grateful to Almighty God for our civil and religious liberty, and taking into our serious consideration the best means of establishing a good Constitution in this State for the sure foundation and more permanent security thereof, declare:

Art. 36. That as it is the duty of every man to worship God in such manner as he thinks most acceptable to Him, all persons are equally entitled to protection in their religious liberty; wherefore, no person ought by any law to be molested in his person or estate, on account of his religious persuasion, or profession, or for his religious practice, unless, under the color of religion, he shall disturb the good order, peace or safety of the State, or shall infringe the laws of morality, or injure others in their natural, civil or religious rights; nor ought any person to be compelled to frequent, or maintain, or contribute, unless on contract, to maintain, any place of worship, or any ministry; nor shall any person, otherwise competent, be deemed incompetent as a witness, or juror, on account of his religious belief; provided, he believes in the existence of God, and that under His dispensation such person will be held morally accountable for his acts, and be rewarded or punished therefore either in this world or in the world to come Nothing shall prohibit or require the making reference to belief in, reliance upon, or invoking the aid of God or a Supreme Being in any governmental or public doc- ument, proceeding, activity, ceremony, school, institu- tion, or place.

Virginia Constitution of 1872:

> *We, therefore, the delegates of the good people of*
> *Virginia, elected and in convention assembled,*
> *in pursuance of said acts, invoking the favor and*
> *guidance of Almighty God, do propose to the people the*
> *following constitution and form of government for this*
> *commonwealth:*
>
> *That religion, or the duty which we owe to our Creator,*
> *and the manner of discharging it, can be directed only*
> *by reason and conviction, not by force or violence; and,*
> *therefore, all men are equally entitled to the free exer- cise*
> *of religion according to the dictates of conscience; and*
> *that it is the mutual duty of all to practice Christian*
> *forbearance, love, and charity towards each other.*

The answer to American ills is not big government, big business or big church, but a return to God. America's manifest destiny was re- vealed to Christopher Columbus, a nation modeled after ancient Is- rael with a divine mandate to be a light to the nations. The forces of humanism that are seeking to hijack America's Judeo-Christian heritage must be defeated.

The United States has shown from time to time, in the face of nation- al crisis, that she turned to God, unlike communist countries who had foreclosed the Biblical influence in their culture, they had no one to turn to. Many Americans still believe in God. Divine favor is still with us. God's hand is still upon America.

Today, America is a sole superpower as a testimony of God's blessing because many Americans still have the fear of God. It is no coinci- dence that the evil empire of the former Soviet Union is a thing of the past. It declared that God is dead. Guess who is dead?! America is only invincible under the shadow of the Almighty. Let's keep it there.

The current revival of moral conservatism and religious orthodoxy in America is a panacea and not a true answer. Religious conservatism survived the Roman conquest of Israel and, in modern times, religious orthodoxy survived communism. American moralism is the most deadly enemy of America's manifest destiny. Evangelical formalism with its sound doctrine, ritualism and political activism has a missing dimension vital for the future of America: the living presence of God. We are in a predicament that precedes death. Israel tried in vain to substitute a vital relationship with God with the highest public moralism and legalism. God was not impressed with such external religiosity and moralism. America is following in Israel's footsteps to divine judgment. America is in desperate need of Bible-based spiritual revival for survival.

Chapter Twenty

BIBLICAL BASIS OF AMERICAN CAPITALISM

The heathen nations hate America for being blessed by God. What these nations do not know is that God has rigged up the world economy to bless His own children. The wealth of the godless nations is laid up for the righteous according to God's word:

> *"the wealth of the wicked is laid up for the just"*
> *Proverbs 13:22*

Ever since America began to turn away from God and deny Biblical absolutes, prayer in public schools and rejected her manifest destiny, she has become the biggest debtor nation on earth from the greatest lender nation. She is now 8 trillion dollars in debt. What a tragedy!

It must be understood that the blessings of God are not automatic but covenantal. God is a covenant-keeping God; when we keep his commandments, we are blessed. Jesus said, "to him much is given much is required." We have been entrusted with so much. God has capitalized us with his divine favor and providence for more than 200 years. God's greatest gift to His children is His presence and material blessings is a byproduct. Human tendency is always to focus on the external or on materialism and to trust in wealth and military power, rather than God. We must use our utmost diligence to avoid confrontation with God. Though we are the mighty nation, He is the

Almighty. We must heed the words of our founding fathers and of President Ronald Regean in recent times when he said:

> *"If we ever forget that we are one nation under God then we will be a nation gone under"*

George Washington Said:

> *"It is the duty of all nations, to acknowledge the providence of the Almighty God, to obey his will, to be grateful for his benefits, and humbly to implore his protection and favor."*

Abraham Lincoln said:

> *"It behooves us then to humble ourselves before the offended power to confess our national sins to pray for cleaning and forgiveness."*

If we continue to depart from our manifest destiny that the sovereign God has appointed us, we will be disappointed. Because missing your appointment with destiny always leads to dysfunctionality. When a nation is displaced from its predestined pathway, it looses its inner dynamics to rise above its enemies and problems.

> *"The wicked shall be turned into hell, and all the nations that forget God." Psalm 9:17*

Several times I have quoted this scripture because it is central to the subject matter of this book. We must heed these words of King David, a man after Gods heart, as he warns the future generations of the impending judgment if they turn away from God.

Chapter Twenty-One

THE SPIRITUAL ROOTS OF INDIVIDUALISM AND TRUE CAPITALISM

The construction of the American capitalist system was largely shaped by the great spiritual reawakening which presented the beginning of the age of individualism which broke away from the collective and the status quo of the Old World. The new theology of personal salvation ultimately provided the social framework that advocated for free enterprise. Capitalism intrinsically grew out of the free society that immediately emerged out of the spiritual reformation. Judeo-Christian values created the social environment vital for free enterprise to work.

> *"Then God said, Let Us make man in Our image,*
> *according to Our likeness; let them have dominion over*
> *the fish of the sea, over the birds of the air, and over the*
> *cattle, over all the earth and over every creeping thing*
> *that creeps on the earth." Genesis 1:26*

This revelation of God's will to give man dominion in the marketplace for His glory revolutionized the American mindset. It defined the dignity of work. Human work became a sacred duty to God. Colonial America, in and of itself, could not bring about the economic revolution that followed the great reawakening. Inspiration led to perspiration. The Protestant work ethic made the difference from all other economies in other democracies. The new society that emerged from the spiritual great reawakening embraced such virtues as diligence, integrity, honesty, fairness and equity. They applied more diligence to the task of alleviation of deprivation and suffering caused by social inequities than any other society on earth because of their profound spirituality.

Needless to say, the key element in American prosperity is the stupendous fact that God's infallible promises were realized and fulfilled as a consequence of a whole people in pursuit of their divine manifest destiny. This biblical economic perception was vital in shaping the collective moral cultural structure conducive to free enterprise and democracy.

This Biblical restructuring of the American society affected the life of virtually every person. In general, the American public still tends to inherently believe that America, as a whole, is blessed by God because of this profound transformation of the American ethos that transcended race and ethnicity which emerged out of the great revivals. This is best explained by Benjamin Franklin Morris (1810- 1867), a notable American historian, who wrote in his insightful work, The Christian Life and character of the civil institutions of the United States in 1864 when he said:

> *"This is a Christian nation, first in name and secondly because of many and might elements of pure Christianity which have given it character and shaped its destiny from the beginning. It is pre-eminently the land of the Bible, of the Christian Church, and of the Christian Sabbath.*
>
> *The chief security and glory of the Untied States has been, is now and will be forever the prevalence and domination of the Christian faith."*

It would be preposterous to deny the remarkable faith in God in the American people which resulted in God's mighty hand upon this nation. It is evident from the magnitude of the blessings that God has put upon this nation that it is a sovereign work of God that has made this nation what it is. There is no question about it. All doubt is easily dispelled because there is no other nation with such abundance. It pays to fear God! King David, one of the most powerful kings in Israel, shares this most profound understanding regarding divine providence:

> *"He will bless those who fear the Lord, Both small and*
> *great. May the Lord give you increase more and more.*
> *You and your children. May you be blessed by the Lord,*
> *who made heaven and earth. The heaven, even the*
> *heavens, are the Lord's but the earth He has given to the*
> *children of men." Psalm 115:13-16*

The sad thing today is that America is rapidly departing from its Protestant ethic as a basis of free enterprise and assuming more and more a Darwinian ethic, which solely bases success in business to the survival of the fittest or a technocratic ethic, which advocates performance as the sole reason for success. The negative effect of this moral departure from the Protestant ethic is the indisputable decline of American capitalism.

The American dream is becoming the American nightmare to those being marginalized and victimized by the dog-eat-dog, faceless capitalism which is rapidly replacing compassionate capitalism. It is apparent that the current widening margin between the haves and the have-nots is indicative of the spiritual condition of this nation. Modern America is quickly moving towards ever-increasing economic stagnation because she is explaining away the historical, divine factor as irrelevant and false enchantment.

Historically, public morality ultimately determines the country's economic system and the essence of any culture reveals the fundamental factors which define its economic system. The post- Christian,

European Community's form of capitalism is based upon Darwinian ethic and the result is more and more government intervention and higher and higher taxation for social welfare because of the massive causalities of godless materialism of faceless capitalism.

Europe's Christian foundation has been replaced with secular humanism. This is leading to a gradual death of individualism and a return to the collectivism and paganism of the dark ages. The Chinese, like the Europeans, have no spiritual basis to their form of capitalism. They follow the technocratic ethic and the result is sweatshops and slave labor. The Chinese model offers consumerism without political pluralism. Free enterprise without freedom. Capitalism without compassion. Both the Darwinian and the technocratic ethic dehumanize the individual. Only American capitalism celebrates individuality because of its Protestant ethic.

In spite of the erosion of the protestant ethos, America is great because she still gives equal opportunity to every person since she still believes all men are created equal. Nevertheless, America's Biblical foundation is under virulent attack. Yet she remains resilient because there are still so many people that are still adhering to the Biblical absolutes. God's hand is still upon America. It seems plain, both in retrospect and today, that there are still many Americans that are substantially of the old school; their faith in God takes precedence over everything else. This creates, of course, a reason to hope that the greatest days of America lie ahead. It is true that there is a growing hunger in America to return to her spiritual foundation which I personally believe will restore American capitalism back to a dominant place in the twenty- first century.

Meanwhile, regardless of economic prosperity or lack of it, America needs revival and a return to the basics and fundamentals that made America great. To be sure of a bright future, the root of American hope and optimism for the battle for the survival of this nation must again be found in the notion that was heralded by the founding fathers and best expressed by Patrick Henry:

> *"Give me liberty or give me death… Sir, we are not*
> *weak, if we make proper use of the means which the*
> *God of nature hath placed in our power. Three million*
> *people, armed in the Holy cause of Liberty, and in such*
> *a country as that which we possess, are invincible by any*
> *force which our enemy can send against us. Beside Sir,*
> *we shall not fight our battles alone. There is a just God*
> *who presides over the destinies of nations; and who will*
> *raise up friends to fight our battles for us."*

The fierce battle for autonomous individualism, old time religion, Protestant work ethic and free enterprise in the future of America has begun in earnest. In the light of such, we must retrieve the truth from those who have hidden it beneath an avalanche of lies and mis-interpretation of the origin and basis of American free enterprise. We are facing a terminal crisis. Corporate greed has replaced corporate responsibility and compassion for the needy. The poor are getting poorer and the rich are getting richer. The American dream is becoming more and more the American nightmare for most average people.

We must reclaim America from the forces of consumerism, materialism, and hedonism and godless, dog-eat-dog capitalism based upon Darwinian or technocratic ethic. Compassion and a need to help your poor neighbor must again drive capitalism based upon Protestant ethic. God has made us our brother's keeper. Protestant ethic empowers everybody to participate in the upward mobility and no one is left behind.

Time is of essence. It is incumbent upon you to accelerate the struggle against the forces of evil and stop the snowball factor of the destruction of the foundational truth undergirding the moral structures of our free society. It is time to take a closer look at what's going on in America—corporate meltdown, bankruptcies, stock market crashes, debt implosion and insolvency of multinationals—all because of adopting a Darwinian and technocratic business ethic foreign to our founding fathers. These current economic events have a message which we ignore at our own peril. While these events are viewed by many as classical economic cycles and natural adjustments, there is more to these current events that demands our serious attention. Jesus said, "The love of money is the root of all evil." At the core of our problems is the love of money. America cannot serve two gods of mammon and God. The sad thing is the fact that the church has adopted the Darwinian ethic in its pursuit of power and fame. It is now a case of the blind leading the blind. Great nations have been raised by God in the past and are now gone because of their rebellion against divine absolutes. America must learn from the past and avoid the historical pitfalls.

The election of America as a special nation with a unique role in history makes it imperative to examine current events in the light of our history and not in comparison to other nations with no Biblical manifest destiny. America was framed by Christian theology. The disproportionate prosperity of America in the world arises undeniably from the faith of the founding fathers in God. It is this fact that transformed seemingly ordinary people from all over the world into a formidable nation. A few years ago, it was remarkable to see how the American private sector leveraged its historical religiosity to bounce back to its spiritual roots after 9-1-1. America, as a nation, returned to her God with prayer all across the land. Looking around the nation, there appears to be an inherent equilibrium between the Christian conservatives and the liberals. The scale could swing to the left in this decade if the silent majority does not stand up and be counted at this crisis hour. Time to act is now! The battle is raging for the future of this nation. The liberal agenda must be defeated.

Widespread complacency and false assumptions that American's economy will never collapse threatens serious consequences that could unravel and shatter our economy if we continue to adapt the Darwinian business ethic. Capitalism requires spiritual capital. God is the author of economic growth and prosperity.

> *"And you shall remember the Lord your God, **for it is
> He who give you power to get wealth,** that He may
> establish His covenant which He swore to your fathers,
> as it is this day." Deuteronomy 8:18*

If America is to reach its highest potentiality in the twenty first century, she must have a deeper appreciation of divine providence in her history. Only through a more penetrating perception of what God has done, from the discovery of the New World to this day, can we go forward and realize our highest potentiality. We must understand that America needs a higher view of herself and a refocus on her manifest destiny, lest she drift into a tragedy of epic proportion without God. A genuine understanding of God's hand upon this nation will give an anchor to this generation in an age of uncertainty and ambiguity.

The proponents of an atheistic and materialistic capitalism are deluded by the illusion of short-term economic growth. The sacred scriptures warn us against such presumption.

> *"There is a way which seemeth right unto a man, but
> the end thereof are the ways of death." Proverbs 14:12*

The process of social decay ultimately will eventuate in the inevitable judgement of God. It is not too late! The process can be reversed through repentance and humility before God.

> *"If my people who are called by My name will humble
> themselves, and pray and seek My face, and turn from
> their wicked ways, then I will hear from heaven, and
> will forgive their sin and heal their land."
> 2 Chronicles 7:14*

Chapter Twenty-Two

AMERICA AT THE CROSSROADS

The current absence of moral and spiritual consensus as a framework of western civilization has left America divided, fragmented, and vulnerable to social upheaval and ethic tension.

Historically, American democracy, in this melting pot of pluralistic society, worked because of the Judeo-Christian ethics established by the founding fathers and the framers of the constitution. The removal of American Christian values is undermining the very foundations of this great nation. Protestantism shaped American individualism and optimism. Democracy is an idea that works in a society with a national ethos. Evangelicalism gave America its soul and its manifest destiny. It is the glue that holds the nation together.

In modern history, the Christian faith is profoundly American. Most Americans believe that they are living in a Christian civilization that was founded on Biblical values, that emphasized individualism, morality, practicality, hard work, respect and honor of the country. The early history of America is in intricately woven by the continual, providential intervention that shaped its self-consciousness as one nation under God. The divine plan of God is the only explanation of the rise of America as a superpower from its humble beginnings. This does not negate the human aspects nor obscures the evils of slavery.

There are too many extraordinary coincidences to deny the hand of providence in the founding of this country. America's origin does not belong to great men and women but to the miraculous, sovereign will of God, working through human instrumentality.

We must return to the manifest destiny of the New World as envisioned by Christopher Columbus in his original vision: the land where the gospel will be carried to the nations of the world in the last days. A chosen people for a divine mission to the nations. A holy people, blessed to be a blessing to the world.

One cannot fail to see the divine design underlying the beginnings of this nation. This is a story rarely told. Yet there is no more exciting, gripping and inspiring story anywhere in modern history as incredible as the hand of providence throughout American history. This is why the Pilgrims had unshakeable convictions that America was new Israel.

The Pilgrims, coming out of the inquisition era and its tidal wave of sorrows, persecutions and indescribable inhumanity and suffering for the sake of Christ, came to the new world to create a free society, more merciful, more loving, more torrent, more educated, more humane, more kind, more beautiful and more open, with a Biblical orientation towards a conception of unique manifest destiny.

The founding fathers believed that theirs was a holy and sacred mission and that God was on their side. They left the hate-filled Old World of indifference with a vision of a land free from religious persecution.

The reason for studying history is because history repeats itself. History foretells the future. America is chosen, though it is backslidden. Yet there is still a deep-rooted feeling of being Gods special people, unique among the family of nations. There cannot be a more important issue today than a serious look at Isreal's historical landscape to understand America's predicament as a chosen people.

America is at the crossroads. She is struggling to stay the course. America is suffering from the same classic problems that ancient Israel experienced: too blessed to be thankful decived that materialism and military power makes a nation indivisible. America's shift towards secularism is creating an idea that America is no man's land, a pluralistic democracy, a melting pot, without a unique national ethos or manifest destiny.

The American people are experiencing a national identity crisis for the first time. The erosion of Christian values is undermining national unity and oneness as a diverse people yet one united by a common manifest destiny and Judeo-Christian heritage.

The alarming erosion of Judeo-Christian values and the discarding of Biblical absolutes is causing America to fall apart into ethnicity, class struggle and racial conflict because there is no center to hold the country together.

Undeniably, this has a profound effect on the future of the world because, if America goes, the whole world will collapse. The bogus values of materialism will not sustain America in the face of impending forces of evil seeking to destroy the American republic. We need more than reformation for survival–we need revival.

If one looks at the present tension between the demonizing influences of secularism, the signs are everywhere that things will not continue to remain the same. Something has gone wrong in America. She is sick and dying. The myth that America, stripped of its divine man- ifest destiny, will stand against the forces of evil seeking to destroy this nation will prove delusional as the history of ancient Israel has already proved.

> *"For the nation or kingdom that will not serve God will perish; it will be utterly ruined." Isaiah 60:12*

History is full of examples of nations that forgot God, and today they are on the garbage heap of the ages. The global changes we are facing require that we return to the fundamentals that made this nation great. This is an extraordinary era. There are troubling similarities between ancient Israel's predicament before divine judgment and America's today.

We must look beneath the surface of the current crisis to identify the deeper causes. The free world is suffering from an epidemically corrupt, spiritual alienation from God, moral breakdown and a loss of purpose and direction. These social ills are indicative of the impending judgment.

Evangelicalism is slowly dying and becoming more and more irrelevant because it has lost its power from on high. The church needs to move beyond social activities as a panacea for lack of true spirituality.

The rise of America a sole superpower at the end of the cold war emboldened the American people to believe in themselves rather than in God. This poses a greater danger to the future of the republic as one nation under God than the cold war or Islamic extremism and international terrorism.

It is time to focus on ourselves and our own crisis of moral erosion taking place at an alarming rate, which will inevitably crash this country if we do not act now. Today, ethnicity and competing pluralistic interests groups are pulling the nation apart. The house divided will not stand. America is too vulnerable to international terrorism, ethnic cleansing, religious fanatics, drug lords, compound debt crisis and declining economic production coupled with a global energy crisis. Only God can sustain America as a sole superpower. We need, now more than ever before, to restore unity as one nation under God. It is time to restore our manifest destiny.

I cannot help but fear that America is heading towards the same path as the former godless evil empire of the Soviet Union because of the current religious decline. The fuse has already been lit. The spiritual condition in our country has a chilling effect on all God-fearing Americans. The globalists in our country, impelled out of the cold war with new gusto, are seeking to establish a godless democracy as the New Hope for the New World Order.

The globalization of American idealism without God at the center will only lead to a predictably defunct utopia.

Such a utopia will collapse at the convergence of spiritual and economic factors precipitated by global monopolies, marginalized masses in under developed countries and irrational delusions of religious fanatics seeking to obtain weapons of mass destruction to destroy everything in the name of God.

The net effects of the amalgamation of global terrorism, corporate corruption, moral erosion, materialism and secularism engenders a phenomena that precedes the death of western civilizations if America does not heed the call of God to repentance and rekindle its passion to bear the light of Christ to the nations.

It is particularly incumbent upon the God-fearing, country-loving, law-abiding silent majority in this country to stand up and fight the forces of evil and reclaim and retrieve America's manifest destiny for future generations.

Unless America embraces again the Biblical principles of integrity, hard work, tenacity and ingenuity, which embodied the legacy of the founding fathers, this country will decline into a third-world democracy in our generation.

Recent events in our country point to testing days ahead of us as the threat of terrorism, economic downturn, corporate depravity and national uncertainty continues to grow. Judging the future from the recurrent market volatility and unprecedented market gyrations, the bear and the bull market circles have become more and chaotic and unpredictable. God is speaking to us both on Wall Street and Main Street. We see signs of the times on every side.

To think that America will remain a sole superpower, apostatized and rebellious against God, is illusionary thinking. The moral and God-fearing majority are just delaying their defeat unless they stand up now and be counted. The hour has come to fight for America on our knees in prayer.

The heightened tension between fundamentalism and liberalism has to do with evangelical objection to sodomy, same-sex marriage, abortion and condoms on demand in our high schools. Evangelical legalism cannot defeat human depravity. The fundamentalists are stigmatized for adhering to Biblical absolutes as a moral standard for America. The moral agenda is dividing America.

The question is, who has the right to define the moral standard of this nation? God has the right to set the moral standard for mankind.

He did it! He wrote it in the Bible. America must adhere to God's word and Jesus Christ. History shows us clearly that Biblical absolutes alone failed to transform nations; only the grace of God can through the person of the Lord Jesus working in human nature. Needless to say, human depravity cannot be the basis of social, moral standards as advocated by the liberal left. The freedoms enshrined in the American Constitution do not constitute freedom from God's moral standard.

The liberal left wants to interpret America's freedom as freedom to change the law of God. The church, as the light bearer, is called to not be neutral in matters of morality. The church has a divine imperative to declare the law of God at the public square and to raise the moral standard for the nation. Needless to say, this does not constitute a mandate for the moral majority to force individuals to live by the Biblical moral standard in their private life. Nevertheless, public morality defined by the Creator must be maintained and observed in public affairs. The laws of the country, without interfering with people's private lives, must be upheld. There has to be a balance. People must be free to do what they want in privacy—that is God's sphere of oversight. No government has the right to control the private deeds of its citizens. Governments must control public morality. This is their prerogative. Public moral standard must be defined by the Ten Commandments given by the Creator. The private sphere belongs to God.

The social crisis we are facing in America today is a result of the changing moral code from a Bible-based, infallible bedrock of God's law to the ever-shifting sand of transitory values of situational ethics of the "me" generation. The danger that I see in America today is that the people of God are retreating from the battle for the future of America's public morality and acquiescing in the name of American freedom. This is a tragic failure that will destroy the future generations and rob them of their inheritance as one nation under God.

As America continues to move more and more towards the left and the liberals are taking control of the public square, the consequences are incomprehensible. We are already seeing an alarming increase in crime, abortion on demand, school shootings, drug addiction and sodomy.

The battle for the future of America's manifest destiny is being threatened not by international terrorism but by the death of the family unit. America is a tottering giant on the verge of internal collapse. If we do not learn from history, it will repeat itself. The Roman Empire collapsed because of moral decay. No nation ever survived moral decay. We are our own enemies.

We must confront these forces of evil within our society attempting to rob America of its manifest destiny. The time has come to reclaim this nation and its social institutions back to its past greatness.

The America we all love, which brought the pilgrims to the shores of this country to face great hardships with a hope of building a Bible-based civilization, must be restored. We must become again a lighthouse to the sea of humanity. The envy of the entire world, champions globally of everything that is lovely and beautiful in man: the America that is worth saving for our grandchildren. The time has come to put a stop to the systematic removal of scriptural values and its replacement with situational ethics in society. The pilgrims came to America in search of a place where they could exercise freedom of conscience and religious freedom and not freedom from religion.

Today, no matter where you look, you are confronted with a sad state of unbridled godlessness and all manner of human perversion. There is such an alarming rise in preteen pregnancies, rampant child abuse, condom distribution in public schools, kiddie porn, same-sex marriage, divorce and juvenile crime. These formidable, internal enemies of anything that is good and moral rip the nation apart.

America is heading toward a moral showdown. America is divided! The conservative and the liberals are on a collision course. The left wants to dismantle the America of the founding fathers piece by piece. They are leading a cultural coup d'état, while, at the same time, the external enemies are planning our demise.

America is at the crossroads in every aspect. Many of our old standards and shared assumptions and experiences, such as respect for the rule of law based upon Biblical absolutes, are gone. The Ten Commandments are being removed from the public square. Christ as the reason for Christmas is being removed; prayer in public schools is now illegal. Jesus is no longer a welcome guest in the institutions that were built for His glory. America is spiritually weak and it is headed towards the natural death as a great nation. America's sickness is reaching a crisis point.

Chapter Twenty-Three

AMERICA'S CULTURAL CRISIS

I am writing this chapter while sitting in a hotel in New York near ground zero. I believe 911 is indicative of the fact that heaven's shield is being lifted away from us. America is facing a terminal crisis of moral depravity. The religious right in the 80s and 90s sensed that the nation was on the wrong path to decline and decay. They called America back to conservative humanism, or traditional values, in vain. The counteraction to the moral majority revolution is escalating the disintegration of the American family and the crisis of identity.

The new right has not saved America's soul and cannot because only God can change the human heart. Christian political action has not restored America to its greatness. There is no hope in the Christian right. They have no answers. They have ambition and no vision. The demise of their great nation continues at an overwhelming pace while they are spending millions on panacea. The dilemma of modern American society is more complex than the simple return to traditional values. The restoration of moral absolutes delineates an impossible task. America needs God! We need a true cure to our ills: Jesus Christ.

The conservative agenda, or its contract with America, only suppresses the problem in America. It cannot solve it. It is like denying you have cancer when you are sick and dying. The coalition of conservative humanism and evangelical moralism would have you believe that you can simply deny that the cancer exists by returning to looking good again. Dress up the problem! Cover up the problem!

Hide it! America is dying. It is demoralized and defeated. It is on a pathway to dismal pessimism and destruction. The glory of God upon America has succumbed to shameful, disgraceful and terrible malaise. A booming economy has opiated the people while the nation is plunging into the abyss of moral decay.

The world plummets towards chaos with America at the pinnacle of its power as a world leader and sole superpower–precariously skewed, impotent and irrelevant. America is experiencing prosperity without purpose, which is the most perilous predicament. The American grandeur and its prestigious institution of past glory will be reduced to ashes and rubble. The death of America poses terminal danger to Western civilization because she is not discerning her time of visitation. God has an appointment with America. Religious fundamentalism, political conservatism and moral re-orientation will not save this nation. Even today's unparalleled prosperity will not save us from falling into the bottomless black hole. We are living on borrowed time.

We must learn from history. A mighty wave of reformation and conservatism is a vain attempt to do what only God can do! We need prayer. We need God! Things are worse now than ever before. Moral standards are at the lowest ebb. The middle class is being squeezed out. Most people in America today live hand to mouth. The poor are being exploited. The deficit is getting higher and higher each year. Abortion is on the rise. More than fifty percent of Christian marriages end up in divorce. The American family is dying. HIV cases are rising at an alarming rate in the American ghetto. Our diagnosis of the problem is wrong and so is our cure. The left is blaming the right for seeking to do what is right. Both are on the wrong path to the future. The right wants to do what is right without being in right standing with God. The left is dedicated to open rebellion and sodomy.

America's problem is spiritual paralysis. Moral reformation without transformation. Evangelical conservatism and fundamentalism will not restore America's glory. America needs to hear the good news. America needs the power of God. America has lost its vision and therefore its mission. Christopher Columbus clearly states the purpose of this nation in the community of nations as preaching the gospel, not the export of capitalism and democracy. Christ is the hope of the world. American culture has a lot of good things but it is not the answer.

America is a leader with a major problem of not knowing the way to go. She has no plan. As always, when a leader fails to lead, it creates confusion. The Bible says that, without a vision, the people perish. Lack of vision always causes a crisis of leadership. America has no vision. It has the position of power without purpose. Power without a plan corrupts. People do not like to be managed. They want to be led. The world is looking for a leader, not a macro manager. America is being hated for being a global crisis manager rather than a leader with a clear vision.

The moral majority needs a vision greater than its glorious heritage. Each generation must have its own visitation from on high. America is not great because of its founding fathers, or because of its constitution or its separation of Church and State. Greatness comes from God, not from antiquities, precedents, documents and patriotism. It is God who lifts up and puts down. History is only to show us the pathway to new summits of glory.

This land was not discovered by human initiative. God led Columbus. God has a plan for this land. Human plans will not work. If God does not build the house, they that labor, labor in vain. Jesus is the only hope of this nation's rise to new heights of glory.

The religious right will consummate this nation's demise. They will tarnish the church of Jesus Christ. Diminish the church's effectiveness. The church's societal, political activism has marshaled billions of dollars frenetically to save the status quo in vain. This misguided preoccupation with the affairs of this world has left the house of the Lord in shambles and the present spiritual melee that has wrought skyrocketing moral decay and an avalanche of disillusionment and despondency.

Political agenda has replaced God's kingdom agenda. The church, like Israel, is selling its birthright. We are born of God, kings and priests unto our God. We are His ambassadors of the eternal kingdom.

The Gospel of Jesus Christ will save America from the garbage heap of the bygone kingdoms. The gospel must take preeminence again in the church in this land. Traditional conservatism is misleading America and is delusional in its mission. Our Kingdom is not of this world. Save the soul of America and you will save America's greatness. Jesus is the ultimate solution to the human dilemma. America's cherished glory cannot be compared with the glory that God wants to give to this nation by lifting us up to new, dizzying heights of glory if the church would return to the great task of the proclamation of the foolishness of the Gospel of Jesus Christ to this generation.

Social gospel and its call to political action mingled with American pragmatism can only produce a false sense of security. We are building a house on the sand that cannot stand when the storm comes. The present message of the church is not sufficient for the day of visitation. The hour has come to build our house on the rock of ages that was cleft for you. There is a hiding place in God. It is a place of majesty and glory. God is calling America unto Himself, one person at a time.

The problem in our nation is not the proliferation of pornography, abortion, political disarray, injustice, discrimination, disintegration of the family and loss of human rights and privacy, but in rebellion against God. The above symptoms are the signs of a dying church. The church is supposed to be the light of the world and the salt of the earth. The nation is in darkness because the church has lost the f lame for soul-winning and holy living. The church has become part of big government and big business. The prodigal church in this land is in the pigpen, feeding on pigs' leftover garbage from the rich man's table of lavish excesses of moral corruption and unrivaled financial extravagance. The preachers have become servants of big money interests. Prophets for profit! We are in a spiritual predicament that precedes terminal crisis and death.

Chapter Twenty-Four

THIS IS THE HOUR FOR THE CHURCH IN AMERICA

The momentous issue is, how can we reshape this nation to fit and conform to its manifest destiny? The American dilemma is spiritual. The present state of this nation makes the Bible the only handbook for survival. The only hope for the future of this nation is spiritual revival. The church is a sleeping giant at the switch; she must awake and sound the alarm.

> *"Blow the trumpet in Zion: sound the alarm on my holy hill. Let all who live in the land tremble for the day of the Lord is coming it is close at hand—a day of darkness and gloom, a day of clouds and blackness. Like dawn spreading across the mountains, a large and might army comes, such as never was of old nor ever will be in ages to come. Joel 2:1-2*

Christianity has become a way of life without God. The American way! The American culture! The American heritage! Whatever spirituality America experienced during the great re-awakenings has deteriorated into nothingness. The present moral predicament of America is an indictment of empty religiosity of American intelligentsia and its poetic rhetoric on Sundays devoid of power. The church has a form of godliness without substance and reality of the risen Christ.

American idealism permeates the church, rather than the separateness of the called out (ecclesia). The recent history of our nation of the blight of corporate corruption, betrayal, and rampant crime is indicative of a deeper malady deep in the soul of America.

AMERICA IN THE AGE OF DELUSION

Americans are experiencing a moral crisis. More than ever before, this decade is becoming a decade of delusion and alarming moral decline. The delusion is caused by the collapse of the former Soviet Union and the rise of America as the sole superpower in conjunction with the wave of democracy sweeping across the world. Is this the triumph of good over evil and the virtues of free enterprise over the tyranny of communism? Do we stand today at the threshold of the golden age or the darkest hour in history?

The chilling reality is that we are in a predicament that demands bold action. It is becoming more and more obvious that we are facing monumental and unprecedented ecological crisis, political instability and international terrorism that threaten our very survival. The rat race for the creation of weapons of mass destruction continues unabated in barbaric nations. The cold war is being replaced with Islamic fundamentalism as an ideology of confrontation with the free world. Can America survive the coming global energy crisis and global war on terror?

Though America is blessed with vast resources, it is crumbling be- cause its spiritual walls have fallen down. Monetary success will not save a nation from moral depravity. Economic and political bootstraps will not hold this nation together from decadent decline and internal decay.

It's not too late to save America from moral bankruptcy, rampant and pandemic glaring abortion and crime rate.

The stakes are too high for America; she must rise and be a comfort to the people of God worldwide, if she returns to her first love. Will America return to God and rediscover her destiny? Yes, America will rise—one person at a time. This is your hour. You are reading this book by divine appointment.

Our nation needs to make the Lord Jesus supreme in the heart, and to proclaim the good news. Apart from this mission, America has no distinct existence. The weighty matter, which prompted me to write this message, is the nearness of Jesus's return. This nation has a divine mandate to take the whole gospel to the whole world. The tragedy in the common house of mankind is that we, to whom the message of eternal hope has been entrusted, have diluted it and sugar-coated it with meaningless rituals. We have closed the gap between the sacred and the secular and have developed religious expression more in harmony with the free market system. The present religious resurgence has not produced Christians, but moralists. The church is the prodigal son that needs to return home to the Father. Tradi- tional ethical principles based upon Judeo-Christian values are not Biblical Christianity. These values are essential for a free enterprise, market economy but not for salvation and sanctification. Christ must be made paramount again in the hearts of men if America is to fulfill its manifest destiny.

The present condition of the church constitutes a continuum of all that entails the American dream, vastly reduced to worldliness. The world came into the church as the church failed to go out into the world to make disciples. The church, wanting to be acceptable to the world and savoring a position of power and influence, traded its birthright like Esau.

The prodigal church emphasizes dogma rather than a vital relation-ship with Jesus. The Bible demands practical application rather than intellectual ascent and empty belief. Moral do-goodism destroys spir-itual orientation and the effectual working of the Holy Spirit in the guilt-ridden people. Moralism is panacea and not a cure. American moralism is paralyzing the people from a pursuit of God. The rise of religious conservatism and its vision for the reconstruction of Ameri-ca destroys the effectiveness of the gospel of salvation as an act of God in time, space and matter. It provides superficial reformation without transformation of the individual, and is consequently a rationale for rightness without justification by faith alone.

It is apparent that America is groping for a new ethos of ultimate concern. The phenomenal success of our nation in geopolitics as a sole superpower is robbing this nation of its spiritual fervor. Religious conservatism without the Living Christ is an idolatrous alternative to the truth. Commitment to God must be derived from the revelation of the Lord Jesus. American alienation from the God that chose this nation for a unique position in the family of nations will ultimately affect every person on earth. The world is assimilating the American version of Christianity. The new brand of godless Christianity packaged as western civilization and sold successfully on the world market place is becoming more of a mark of assimilation into western civilization rather than a true change of heart. It is becoming an in-thing to look American all over the world. It's a symbol of being part of the civilized and sophisticated. I am not denying that there is a place for Judeo-Christian ethics as a universal moral standard that encourages social justice, yet the most significant aspect of Christianity is Christ in you, the hope of glory. This form of social gospel is relevant for free enterprise but inadequate for salvation and transformation.

God chose America and destined her to be the light to the nations. We are to bring the whole gospel to the whole world. God wants us, as a nation, to be red-hot for Jesus. We will be invincible as long as we remain faithful to God who chose us. President Abraham Lincoln was conscious of this fact when he made this warning to the Ameri- can people;

> *"But we have forgotten God. We have forgotten the gracious hand which preserved us in peace and multiplied and enriched and strengthened us and we have vainly imagined that in the deceitfulness of our hearts, that all these blessings were produced by some superior wisdom and virtue of our own."*

He described our present situation, though American history confronts us with a modern, and most clear-cut, evidence and testimony of God's overwhelming providence, parallel to that of the

Jewish people in ancient times yet, in spite of this eloquent seamless record of divine providence, modern America denies it as coincidental and a myth.

The present, comprehensive reassessment of ourselves does not give us a good picture. Spiritual Revival is indispensable for our survival at this critical juncture in our history. We must deny ourselves and take up our cross and follow Jesus—the way, the truth and the life—whole-heartedly.

Chapter Twenty-Five

GOD'S SOLUTION TO AMERICA'S ECONOMIC CRISIS

God wants to take America to new heights of greatness in this new millennium. The Bible teaches that economic growth is a gift of God to those that obey His covenant laws. Our economic future will be determined by the level of our allegiance and commitment to God and not by Darwinian self- determinism. God is the only determinative factor in our future. This is God's promise to us.

> *"Now it shall come to pass, if you diligently obey the voice of the Lord your God, to observe carefully all His commandments which I command you today, that the Lord your God will set you high above all nations of the earth. And all these blessings shall come upon you and overtake you, because you obey the voice of the Lord your God: Blessed shall you be in the city, and blessed shall you be in the country. Blessed shall be the fruit of your body, the produce of your ground and the increase of your herds, the increase of your cattle and the offspring of your flocks. Blessed shall be your basket and your kneading bowl. Blessed shall you be when you come in, and blessed shall you be when you go out.*

> *The Lord will cause your enemies who rise against*
> *you to be defeated before your face; they shall come out*
> *against you one way and f lee before you seven ways.*
> *The Lord will command the blessing on you in your*
> *storehouses and in all to which you set your hand, and*
> *He will bless you in the land which the Lord your God*
> *is giving you. The Lord will establish you as a holy*
> *people to Himself, just as He has sworn to you, if you*
> *keep the commandments of the Lord your God and walk*
> *in His ways. Then all peoples of the earth shall see that*
> *you are called y the name of the Lord, and they shall be*
> *afraid of you." Deuteronomy 28:1-10*

Those who align themselves with God in sweet fellowship experience His blessings. One thing is sure, the biblical, economic perspective of the founding fathers of America remains the true foundation, capable of ushering us into a new age of unprecedented prosperity in this new millennium.

We have a second chance to restore American capitalism based upon Protestant ethic and compassion for the poor and the under-privileged. America must seize the opportunity and return to Biblical Christianity. The revisionists of American history have no power to stop divine intervention. God is on the side of those who are faithful to his word. Darwinian, technocratic capitalism will fail. It has no power. It is dead. It has no future. The future is on the side of God's people. It is time to take the offensive. Churchill once said:

> *"The hottest places in hell must be reserved for those*
> *who, in the face of great moral crisis, maintain their*
> *neutrality."*

If the moral majority remains silent, America will continue to turn into a Darwinian, socialistic utopia. Materialism and capitalism driven by greed is spreading like cancer. The hour has come to stem its onslaught on compassionate Protestant business ethic. Unusual times call for unusual measures. We are in the countdown to the beginning of the last chapter of true, free enterprise in our country if we remain spiritually dead. We must return to the good, old-time religion of our founding fathers. Christ must become the center of our focus. Present religious formalism must be replaced with reality.

Chapter Twenty-Six

THERE IS HOPE FOR AMERICA

The good news is that the current crisis is bringing the remnant in America back to her Biblical roots. There is too much good in the American people left to cause us to hope for a great future for this nation. We have inherited an enormous, uncompromising and indestructible idealism and faith in God. Through the years, this divine orientation has consistently contributed to our autonomous commitment to stop the forces of evil from engulfing this planet with its totalitarian, collectivist fundamentalism that idealizes criminality. America will continue to rise to the occasion. God will continue to shine His face upon her. These forces of extremism transform evil into good in the name of God and will be defeated. The apostle Paul foretold of this coming conspiracy of evil in the last days when he wrote:

> *"This know also, that in the last days perilous times shall come. For men shall be lovers of their own selves, covetous, boasters, proud, blasphemers, disobedient to parents, unthankful, unholy, without natural affection, trucebreakers, false accusers, incontinent, fierce, despises of those that are good, traitors, heady, high minded, lovers of pleasures more than lovers of God; Having a form of godliness, but denying the power thereof: from such turn away." 2 Timothy 3:1-5*

The remnant in America will triumph over the seed of the serpent; light over darkness and good over evil. These forces of evil are impervious to the obvious, irrefutable fact that God has raised America at a time such as this as His battle-axe. America's unattainable blessings are evidence that attest to God's providence and favor, yet there is a reprehensible unwillingness to consider the divine factor as the only explanation of America's greatness on part of the liberal left and our external enemies. The enemies of our nation believe America is the great Satan. This is what inspires their intractable hatred of the American people. Though the current dimension of the global conflict epitomizes a movement towards terminal conflict, there is nothing to worry about, for greater is He that is in us than He that is in the world. Jesus said, "cheer up, I have overcome the world." "No weapon formed against you shall prosper." All we need is God on our side.

The dilemma we face is whether we are going to embrace our divine destiny or sell our birthright. America is like the story told of an eagle captured and domesticated and, as a result, lost its identity and destiny, caged in the zoo. After sometime the cage was left open and the eagle was free to stay or f ly away yet it chose to stay in bondage. Many die in bondage to contemporary prosperity, feeding on garbage in spiritual exile, yet some will escape back to their destiny in the sky and break away from the status quo. The whole world wants to domesticate and enslave the American people and put them in the zoo like the rest of them. It is not accidental that our symbol is an eagle. The world hates that we are free. We can f ly. We have a destiny in God in the heavens. When America waits upon the Lord, she will f ly like an eagle again to new heights of glory.

> *"Hast thou not known? Hast thou not heard, that the everlasting God, the Lord, the Creator of the ends of the earth, fainteth not, neither is weary? There is no searching of his understanding. He giveth power to the faint: and to them that have no might he increaseth strength. Even the youths shall faint and be weary, and*

> *the young men shall utterly fall: But they that wait upon*
> *the Lord shall renew their strength; they shall mount up*
> *with wings as eagles; they shall run, and not be weary;*
> *and they shall walk, and not faint." Isaiah 40:28-31*

America, it is not too late! The best for this nation is yet to come. Have faith in God. We have victory in Jesus. Heed the words of the prophet Isaiah. Seize this opportunity and act upon this divine invitation.

> *"Arise shine; for the light is come, and the glory of the*
> *Lord is risen upon thee. For, behold, the darkness shall*
> *cover the earth, and gross darkness the people: but the*
> *Lord shall arise upon thee, and his glory shall be seen*
> *upon thee. And the Gentiles shall come to thy light, and*
> *kings to the Brightness of thy rising." Isaiah 60:1-3*

The center point of this book is not the enemies of America, but the God of America and his plan and purpose for this nation in the divine economy. The New York attack was a call to every American to return to God who chose us for greatness. There is a direct correlation between our commitment to God and our accumulative blessings. Therein lay the secrets of America's future unprecedented prosperity.

The fact remains that America is chosen by God. He is able to keep us to the end if we would keep our trust in Him. Tragically, few understand the meaning and impact of this truth. It is time to catch a fresh glimpse of our awesome and glorious God-given destiny to be a light to the nations. This is a challenge that, once taken, will restore our greatness, reshape our priorities and revitalize our vision in the aftermath of the New York attack. The future of this nation belongs to those who believe in America's manifest destiny.

America shall rise again in God. Like an eagle, she will soar to new heights of glory in Christ. We have reached the zenith of our greatness after the collapse of the former Soviet Union when America became the sole superpower. We must learn from history and not repeat the mistakes in history. Is America on the brink of collapse? Is the catastrophe in New York and the current economic meltdown a signal of the approaching endgame? There is a way out of our current dilemma if we remember that we are what we are by the grace of God and heed his word:

"But thou shalt remember the Lord thy God: for it is he that giveth thee power to get wealth, that he may establish his covenant which he sware unto thy fathers, as it is this day." Deuteronomy 8:18

God has given corporate America this power for the purpose of fulfilling America's manifest destiny, to finance global saturation evangelism and to make known God's holy covenant to the nations.

Chapter Twenty-Seven

A BRIGHT NEW DAY FOR AMERICA

The convergence in America of ancient Solomonic outposts in the New World, unprecedented historical providence and unattainable current aff luence and influence constitute a tapestry of extraordinary divine favor unparalleled in the common house of mankind. The current struggle between America's manifest destiny and the "Refuseniks" to America's divine call as a sole superpower constitute an inescapable conspiracy to destroy America's dominance in the global village. The rationale of our enemies is the rejection of America's claim to choiceness. These forces of evil also hate America's commitment to liberate the world's oppressed masses and to bring the light of the gospel to the dark and lost world.

This is a defining moment for America in the aftermath of 911. In the past, from Christopher Columbus's incredible voyages to the New World, the struggles of the early settlers, the pilgrims, the war of independence, the Civil War, World War I, World War II, the Korean and Vietnam wars, one cannot fail to see genuine chronicles of astonishing, actual events in which God intervened and saved this nation. These are God's footprints in American history that clarify the American distinctiveness and manifest destiny from inception to the present sole superpower status in geopolitics.

The enemies of America's manifest destiny are intensifying their attack while the moral majority continue in vain their long, shameful ways of trying to save America through moral reformation or evangelical legalism without Christ, religion without relationship with God, conformity without transformation, grace without absolutes, salvation without regeneration, satisfaction without sanctification, self- righteousness without right-standing with God, goodness without godliness, rationality without revelation, social gospel without spirituality, conversion without confession of sin, Christianity without Christ, formalism without the formation of Christ in the heart, ritualism without reality and political correct gospel without the cross. This feel-good religion that promotes happiness without holiness is doomed to fail the American people in this crisis hour. These prophets for profit, moneychangers and lovers of filthy lucre are leading America into the garden path of self-destruction.

Time is running out while we are playing games. Our enemies are constant, consistent and dedicated to the single task of humiliating America as one nation under God. We are up against formidable, inherently and brutally evil forces. Our war on terror is a potential tinderbox for an all-out war of apocalyptic proportion, especially in the light of hostile regimes' quest to obtain weapons of mass destruction.

Sad to say though, we are facing a monumental, complex and extraordinary onslaught from our enemies and we are more and more vulnerable because we are apostatized. Yet I believe that it is not too late to turn to God with all our hearts and triumph over our enemies like Israel of old.

A great morrow awaits America, a bright new morning begins today, with you committing to a quality of life and a way of being, becoming of a chosen people, begotten of God, through the person of the Lord Jesus, and as posterity of the pilgrims, who came to the New World to seek a land where they could serve God freely.

America will be changed one person at a time. The pathway back to our manifest destiny is still open. A journey of a thousand miles begins with one step towards the destination, a decision. You can make this a decisive moment in your life's journey, so powerful that it becomes a touchstone for everything you do from now on to restore

America's greatness as one nation under God. Pass this book to some-one else or tell somebody about it. Start a revolution! Make a stand for God; draw a line in the sand. Contend for the faith of our fathers.

A radical shift in our nation towards a more Biblical orientation from consumerism will defeat these forces of evil undermining our divine manifest destiny. Time is of essence; we are living in a predicament that precedes death. Many perils threaten our future. We are stand- ing today at the crossroads: double minded and spiritually paralyzed. Consequently, America is in a terminal dilemma that demands an immediate verdict.

> *"I call heaven and earth to witness this day against you that I have set before you life and death, the blessings and the curses: therefore choose life that you and your descendants may live. And may love the Lord your God, obey His voice, and cling to Him. For He is your life and the length of your days, that you may dwell in the land which the Lord gave to your fathers."*
> *Deuteronomy 30:19-20*

Chapter Twenty-Eight

AMERICAN AIRLIFT OF JEWS FROM ISRAEL DURING THE COMING HOLOCAUST IN THE END OF DAYS

> *"When the dragon saw that he had been hurled to the earth, he pursued the woman who had given birth to the male child. The woman was given **the two wings of a great eagle**, so that she might fly to the place prepared for her in the desert, where she would be taken care of for a time, times and half a time, out of the serpent's reach." Revelation 12:13-14*

In the coming holocaust in the end of time, the Islamic hordes and their allies will seek to destroy the Modern State of Israel and carry out Hitler's final solution to the Jewish problem. America will again come to her aid as part of her manifest destiny in the last days. The woman in this prophecy is Israel that gave birth to Jesus Christ the Savior. The "two wings of a great eagle" is an American airlift of Jews out of extermination in the final jihad or holy war. The apocalyptic literature, with amazing, precise identification, again reveals that the nation with the national symbol of two wings of an eagle, which is America, will rescue the Jews in their hour of crisis. America has a great prophetic future. John's predictions in 90 AD are compatible with Isaiah's prophecy about America given in 700 BC. What these prophetic perceptions portend for the future of America is yet to be seen.

It is a matter of absolute importance that such predictions must be understood beforehand if there is to be a realistic appraisal of these prophecies. One must recognize that these predictions do not exist in a vacuum; time and again real, literal fulfillments have taken place in this dimension of time, space and matter to authenticate their validity. True prophecy must be supported by empirical evidence. In contrast to human think-tank prognostications that have never come to pass, these ancient predictions have never failed. Historical evidence exists to provide us a prophetic benchmark for the future.

There is an indisputable, direct and obvious correlation between the American manifest destiny and these ancient predictions. The current global upheaval must challenge us to a virtual consensus that America should move away from an ideological framework to a theological paradigm if we are to survive at the top. Historical observation indicates the transcendence of providence in every aspect of American history took place when America humbled herself before God.

The impending battle of Armageddon according to the ancient predictions from the sacred writings will be precipitated after the land for peace deal in Israel fails to resolve the Jerusalem issue. Jerusalem will become the tinderbox that will ignite a flame that will consume the whole world in the end of days.

> *"I am going to make Jerusalem a cup that sends all the surrounding peoples reeling. Judah will be besieged as well as Jerusalem. On that day, when all the nations of the earth are gathered against her, I will make Jerusalem an immovable rock for all the nations. All who try to move it will injure themselves."*
> *Zechariah 12:2-3*

This future prophetic dimension contains the largest and most important test for our nation. To better circumscribe these alarming prophetic prospects inherent in our Middle East involvement, it is already apparent that it is the theater of the impending geopolitical confrontation between the superpowers because of the coming global energy crisis. The hour for a major Middle East confrontation is near. It is well known that the Chinese and the Russians desire to dominate the Persian gulf for economic reasons, while the Arabs are seeking their military assistance to destroy the modern state of Israel against the will of the Americans, who regard Israel as their only democratic ally in the sea of dictatorships.

The coming climatic moment in history belongs to God. It is written. Victory is preordained for his people. America has shown time and again, in the face of national crisis, an optimistic presumption that God was on their side. Past experience points overwhelmingly to divine providence in these times of need.

The plan and purpose of God for America will be fulfilled in spite of world opposition, because He keeps His promise to His people as Paul declared in his letter:

> *"The one who calls you is faithful and he will do it"* 1
> *Thessalonians 5:24*

God is committed to America's glorious future, but are you?

Re-embrace your destiny while there is still time. Great days lie ahead of you. This is your hour of decision! Fight for America's manifest destiny because, for this purpose, you were born.

Join the up rising to restore America back to God.
www.theup-rising.com

SCRIPTURE REFERENCES

CHAPTER ONE

1. Daniel 2:21
2. Psalm 9:17

CHAPTER TWO

1. 2 Chronicles 7:14
2. Psalm 9:17

CHAPTER FIVE

1. Ecclesiates 3:15
2. Genesis 12:3
3. Joshua 1:3
4. 4. 1 Kings 10:22-23
5. 5. 1 Kings 4:29-34
6. Isaiah 40:22
7. Ecclesiastes 1:7
8. Exodus 28:30
9. Leviticus 8:8
10. Numbers 27:21 11. 1 Kings 7:48-50
11. 12. 1 Chronicles 28:11-12 & 19
12. 13. Isaiah 46:10

CHAPTER SIX

1. 1. Joshua 1:3

CHAPTER SEVEN

2. Ecclesiastes 3:15
3. Isaiah 18:1
4. Isaiah 66:19
5. Jonah 1:3
6. Jeremiah 10:9

CHAPTER EIGHT

1. 1. Acts 13:22
2. 1 Kings 2:45
3. 2 Chronicles 1:7-12
4. 1 Kings 4:34
5. Romans 11:29
6. Zephaniah 3:10
7. Ecclesiastes 3:15
8. Deuteronomy 7:9

CHAPTER NINE

1. 1. Psalm 37:23

CHAPTER TEN

1. Leviticus 23:4

CHAPTER ELEVEN

1. 1. Romans 8:28

CHAPTER TWELVE

1. Isaiah 40:22
2. Isaiah 18:1-2

CHAPTER THIRTEEN

1. 1. Isaiah 18:7

CHAPTER FOURTEEN

1. Genesis 17:8
2. Jeremiah 31:35-37

CHAPTER FIFTEEN

1. Hosea 2:23
2. Colossians 2:17 3. Exodus 14:9-16
3. 1 Corinthians 15:46
4. Galatians 3:29
5. Leviticus 25:10-11
6. Daniel 7:4

CHAPTER SIXTEEN

1. Deuteronomy 7:6-9
2. Matthew 5:14
3. Revelation 1:6

CHAPTER SEVENTEEN

1. 1. Joshua 23:15-16
2. 2. 2 Chronicles 9:22-28

CHAPTER EIGHTEEN

1. Isaiah 59:2-4
2. 2 Timothy 3:1-7
3. Ezekiel 8:18
4. 2 Chronicles 7:14

CHAPTER NINETEEN

1. Psalm 9:17
2. Galatians 6:7

CHAPTER TWENTY

1. Proverbs 13:22
2. Psalm 9:17

CHAPTER TWENTY-ONE

1.   1. Genesis 1:26
2.   2. Psalm 115:13-16
3.   Deuteronomy 8:18
4.   Proverbs 14:12
5.   2 Chronicles 7:14

CHAPTER TWENTY-TWO

1.   1. Isaiah 60:12

CHAPTER TWENTY-FOUR

1.   1. Joel 2:1-2

CHAPTER TWENTY-FIVE

1.   1. Deuteronomy 28:1-10

CHAPTER TWENTY-SIX

1.   1. 2 Timothy 3:1-5 2. Isaiah 40:28-31
2.   Isaiah 60:1-3
3.   Deuteronomy 8:18

CHAPTER TWENTY-SEVEN

1.   1. Deuteronomy 30:19-20

CHAPTER TWENTY-EIGHT

1.   Revelation 12:13-14
2.   Zechariah 12:2-3
3.   1 Thessalonians 5:24

BIBLIOGRAPHY

1. *Book of Prophecy*, Christopher Columbus
2. *The Libro de las profecias of Christopher Columbus,* Gainesville : University of Florida Press, 1991
3. *The Puritan Origins of the American Self,* Sacvan Bercovitch, New Haven: Yale University Press, 1975
4. *Magnalia Christi Americana; Or the Ecclesiastical History of New-England;* Cotton Mather
5. *The Voyages of Christopher Columbus,* Decil Jane, New York, 1970
6. *The European Discovery of America,* Samuel Eliot Morison
7. *Admiral of the Ocean Sea,* Samuel Eliot Morison
8. *America B.C.,* Barry Fell
9. *Sand and Stars: The Jewish Journey Through Time From The Second Temple To The Sixteenth Century,* Yaffa Ganz
10. *America VC*
11. *Handbook of Biblical Chronology,* Jack Finegan
12. *Why Geography Matters,* Harm de Blij
13. *Europe After Democracy,* Arthur H. Brown
14. Josephus Whiston
15. *Holy Land in Maps,* Ariel Tishby
16. *Diaspora...Am Inquiry into the Contempory Jewish World,* Howard M. Sachar
17. *The Timetables of Jewish History: A Chronology of the Most Important People and Events in Jewish History,* Judah Gribetz
18. *Middle East Conflict,* Mitchell G. Bard
19. *The Light and the Glory,* Peter Marshall and David Manuel
20. *America's Right Turn,* Richard Viguerie and David Franke

21. *On This Day in America,* Wayman
22. *The Great Compromise,* Greg Laurie
23. *America's Real War,* Rabbi Daniel Lapin
24. *His Own Book of Privileges,* Christopher Columbus
25. *This Nation Under God,* Charles E. Kistler
26. *American Slavery,* – Morgan
27. *Remarkable Providences: Readings on Early American History,* John Demos
28. *Typology and Early American Literature,* Sacvan Bercovitch
29. *Chronicles of the Pilgrim Fathers,* Alexander Young

SALVATION PRAYER

You can ask Jesus to come into your heart right now. Pray the following prayer, or a similar one. The words you use aren't as important as the meaning that comes from your heart.

> *Jesus, I am a sinner. Thank you for taking my place and dying for my sins. Right now I open the door of my heart and accept you as my Lord and Savior. Thank you for forgiveness and giving me a new life. Help me to be what you want me to be and to live each day for you. Amen.*

www.ingramcontent.com/pod-product-compliance
Lightning Source LLC
Chambersburg PA
CBHW030304130626
46549CB00002B/692